The Modern Language Association of America

Approaches to Teaching
Masterpieces of World Literature

Joseph Gibaldi, Series Editor

Approaches to Teaching Camus's *The Plague*

Edited by

Steven G. Kellman

The Modern Language Association of America
New York   1985

Copyright © 1985 by The Modern Language Association of America

Library of Congress Cataloging in Publication Data

Main entry under title:

Approaches to teaching Camus's The plague.

(Approaches to teaching masterpieces of world
literature; 6)
    Bibliography: p.
    Includes index.
    1. Camus, Albert, 1913–1960. Peste—Addresses, essays,
lectures.   2. Camus, Albert, 1913–1960—Study and
teaching—Addresses, essays, lectures.   3. Plague in
literature—Addresses, essays, lectures.   4. Algeria
in literature—Addresses, essays, lectures.
I. Kellman, Steven G., 1947–   . II. Series.
PQ2605.A3734P432   1985   843'.914   84-19106
ISBN 0-87352-485-3
ISBN 0-87352-486-1 (pbk.)

Cover illustration of the paperback edition: *Der Doctor Schnabel von Rom: Pestarzt
in einer Schutzkleidung* (1656), copperplate engraving, by Paulus Fürst.

Published by The Modern Language Association of America,
New York, New York

CONTENTS

PREFACE TO THE SERIES

In *The Art of Teaching* Gilbert Highet wrote, "Bad teaching wastes a great deal of effort, and spoils many lives which might have been full of energy and happiness." All too many teachers have failed in their work, Highet argued, simply "because they have not thought about it." We hope that the Approaches to Teaching Masterpieces of World Literature series, sponsored by the Modern Language Association's Committee on Teaching and Related Professional Activities, will not only improve the craft—as well as the art—of teaching but also encourage serious and continuing discussion of the aims and methods of teaching literature.

The principal objective of the series is to collect within each volume different points of view on teaching a specific literary work, a literary tradition, or a writer widely taught at the undergraduate level. The preparation of each volume begins with a wide-ranging survey of instructors, thus enabling us to include in the volume the philosophies and approaches, thoughts and methods of scores of experienced teachers. The result is a sourcebook of material, information, and ideas on teaching the subject of the volume to undergraduates.

The series is intended to serve nonspecialists as well as specialists, inexperienced as well as experienced teachers, graduate students who wish to learn effective ways of teaching as well as senior professors who wish to compare their own approaches with the approaches of colleagues in other schools. Of course, no volume in the series can ever substitute for erudition, intelligence, creativity, and sensitivity in teaching. We hope merely that each book will point readers in useful directions; at most each will offer only a first step in the long journey to successful teaching. We may perhaps adopt as keynote for the series Alfred North Whitehead's observation in *The Aims of Education* that a liberal education "proceeds by imparting a knowledge of the masterpieces of thought, of imaginative literature, and of art."

Joseph Gibaldi
Series Editor

PREFACE TO THE VOLUME

Daru, protagonist in the frequently anthologized story "L'Hôte" ("The Guest"), is Albert Camus's portrait of the teacher as alienated and feckless. A European inculcating French culture in a remote, isolated North African schoolhouse, Daru, like his creator, is at odds with both the worlds that have shaped him. The narrative's final lines proclaim, "Dans ce vaste pays qu'il avait tant aimé, il était seul" 'In this vast land he had loved so much, he was alone.'

This volume is a modest attempt at overcoming the professional solitude of the instructor who uses Camus's second published novel. It is no bravura performance in hermeneutics, deconstruction, or biographical revision. It will shift no paradigms, demolish no systems. Like Donne's canonized love, a book on approaches to teaching Camus's text will not add one more to the plaguey bill. Instead, like Dr. Bernard Rieux's painstaking "chronicle," it attempts simply to bear witness to some collective experiences, to what goes on in classrooms throughout North America when selected teachers and students confront *The Plague*. It may reveal some tricks of the trade to novice and old dog alike, and it may, as well, contribute a tonic *esprit de profession*.

The Modern Language Association has inaugurated its series Approaches to Teaching Masterpieces of World Literature with volumes on such venerable fixtures in the literary firmament as *The Canterbury Tales*, *The Divine Comedy*, *Don Quixote*, and *Beowulf*. In their exalted company, *The Plague* should be as ill at ease as Camus himself was among the Parisian intellectuals who seemed to befriend him when he left Algeria. Although widely studied and respected, Camus's 1947 novel is by no means assured of a permanent niche in the Western pantheon. Not the least of the merits of using *The Plague* as a teaching text is precisely in the opportunity, for both student and teacher, to examine the process of canonization, how and why decisions are made on the agenda for publication, study, and research. Perhaps a direct examination of *The Plague* is less likely to be deterred by genuflection than is the study of an incontrovertible masterpiece. As Germaine Brée notes in her introduction, despite, and because of, a Nobel Prize in literature, Camus's reputation has fluctuated dramatically. And the position of *The Plague* within the Camus œuvre remains problematic. Perhaps this project can convey some of the excitement of confronting in the classroom a text about which the jury is still out, and scrapping.

Of all modern authors in languages other than English, perhaps none, excepting Hermann Hesse, has aroused so much general and enduring enthusiasm among North Americans, especially students, as Albert Camus. The generation that came of age reading *Catcher in the Rye*, *Lord of the Flies*, and *Catch-22* also devoured *The Stranger*, *The Plague*, and *The Fall*, not because the books were assigned in school—often they were not—but because they seemed to address the most urgent issues of personal and social identity. Since its publication in 1948, one year after *La Peste*, the French original, the Random House paperback edition of *The Plague* has never been out of print and has been averaging solid annual sales of 33,000. In American graduate schools, *La Peste* is on the required reading list for 46.7% of the M.A. programs and 53.8% of the Ph.D. programs in French (Campbell 596). But it is probably on the undergraduate level and under such disparate rubrics as English, humanities, comparative literature, history, philosophy, political science, even medicine and law that *The Plague* is now most commonly encountered.

To the teachers in such programs I owe my primary debt for the preparation of this volume. Their generous and thoughtful comments form the basis for many valuable suggestions in part 1, "Materials." And I am especially grateful to those instructors and scholars of *The Plague* who agreed to furnish the essays that constitute part 2, "Approaches." Robert W. Greene and Alex Szogyi read and generously commented on the original manuscript. The Modern Language Association in general and specifically its Committee on Teaching and Related Professional Activities provided sponsorship and supervision. In particular, Joseph Gibaldi, general editor of the series, richly deserves recognition for his encouragement, advice, and effort.

Steven G. Kellman

Part One

MATERIALS

Steven G. Kellman

Editions

Camus's apotheosis as a major author, what Baudelaire would call *un phare* 'a beacon,' was demonstrated not only by his selection for a Nobel Prize but also by the publication of his *Œuvres complètes* in a definitive two-volume edition in the superb Bibliothèque de la Pléiade series. *La Peste* is in volume 1, *Théâtre, Récits, Nouvelles,* edited by Roger Quilliot; volume 2, also edited by Quilliot, is *Essais.* Although a hefty 2,090 pages, the Pléiade volume of fiction does not include *La Mort heureuse,* which was an early avatar of *L'Etranger* and was first published, posthumously, in 1971. Nor does it contain *Le Premier Homme,* the novel on which Camus was working at the time of his death, in 1960, and the fragmentary manuscript that his heirs refuse to release for publication. But it does feature a valuable critical apparatus, including variant readings, textual commentary, and pertinent letters and notebook entries. It is a handsomely produced and expensive book.

Virtually all instructors who teach *La Peste* in the original report that, for reasons of economy and availability, they use one of two paperback editions: either the Livre de Poche or the Folio version. Particularly for undergraduate courses and for courses that emphasize only one work by Camus, it is more practical to require purchase of one of those two and to urge students to consult supplementary material in a library copy of the Pléiade edition. Between Livre de Poche and Folio, there seems no compelling reason to choose one over the other.

The solitary authorized English translation of the novel was done by Stuart Gilbert and first published, simultaneously by American and British houses, in 1948. *The Plague* is available in a hardcover edition in Random House's Modern Library series and in two paperback editions, also under the Random House imprimatur: one in the Vintage series and the other in the Modern Library College Edition series. The texts of the two paperback editions of Gilbert's translation are identical, except that the Vintage edition curiously omits the epigraph by Daniel Defoe from the preface to volume III of *Robinson Crusoe.* It is, however, slightly less expensive.

Reactions to the Stuart Gilbert version as a translation and as a teaching text range from satisfaction through begrudging acceptance to hostility. It is readily available, inexpensive, and generally accurate and readable. Those who fault it have a variety of quibbles: that it at times flattens the subtle humor of the original, that its Britishisms confuse American students, that it is imprecise just "enough to be annoying," that, in a novel deliberately constructed around the tensions between journalism and belles lettres, it is, ironically, too "literary." One instructor characterizes the Gilbert translation as "venerable" but maintains that it is now time for an annotated critical edition in English.

The Plague is not a lengthy novel, and most instructors assign it in its entirety. For specialized purposes, however, excerpts from *The Plague* have been published in other books. The second edition of Burton F. Porter's *Philosophy: A Literary and Conceptual Approach* includes two conversations between Rieux and Tarrou, from part 2 and part 4, that are self-sufficient in treating important ethical issues. A compendium of Camus's work, *Albert Camus: The Essential Writings*, edited by Robert E. Meagher, contains selections from several texts, including *The Plague*.

Other Works by Camus

It has been argued—e.g., by Fitch (*Narcissistic Text*)—that, in a subtle, covert *retour des personnages*, characters reappear from one Camus text to another. Yet far more than for Balzac, each of the works in Camus's *Comédie absurde* is a fresh start and an autonomous entity. Nevertheless, *The Plague* is often taught within the context of a "major authors" course examining the entire Camus corpus or juxtaposing several of Camus's works with those of a related author, like Jean-Paul Sartre, André Gide, or André Malraux. And the conscientious instructor and student might well become familiar with the other Camus texts, relatively few as they are. Most are readily available— in French and in English, and in paperback as well as in cloth.

Of primary interest to a study of *The Plague* would be the two other novels Camus published: *L'Etranger* (translated in the United States as *The Stranger* and in the United Kingdom as *The Outsider*) and *La Chute* (*The Fall*). Taken together, the three novels demonstrate a fascinating evolution in use of point of view and in the theme of the individual's relation to the community. *La Mort heureuse* (*The Happy Death*) was published posthumously and is to *The Stranger* somewhat as *Stephen Hero* is to *A Portrait of the Artist as a Young Man*: a youthful rehearsal, which the author chose not to publish, of his first novel. Also relevant to *The Plague* are the short stories in *L'Exil et le royaume* (*Exile and the Kingdom*).

For most of his career, Camus was active in the theater, as producer, director, actor, and playwright. Among his plays, *L'Etat de siège* (*State of Siege*) is particularly worthy of attention; an allegory of the plague set in medieval Spain, it was written shortly after Camus's novel on the same theme. Also remarkable is the earlier *Caligula*, an exploration, through the figure of the Roman tyrant, of reactions to barbarous, capricious oppression. *Le Malentendu* (*The Misunderstanding*), unusual in its setting in Central Europe, away from the Mediterranean sun and shore, and *Les Justes* (*The Just Assassins*), based on an actual terrorist episode in czarist Russia, are the other two most familiar plays by Camus. Comparatists might also want

to make use of some of his theatrical adaptations, particularly of Faulkner—
Requiem pour une nonne (*Requiem for a Nun*)—and of Dostoevsky—*Les Possédés* (*The Possessed*).

In reviewing Sartre's *La Nausée*, Camus once wrote, "A novel is never anything but a philosophy expressed in images" (*Essays* 199). Camus took seriously his efforts at discursive prose, and his excursions into philosophy and political science have manifest affinities to what he is trying to accomplish in *The Plague*. *Le Mythe de Sisyphe* (*The Myth of Sisyphus*) was originally published in 1942, but the definitive, augmented edition appeared the year after publication of *La Peste*. It seizes, as an emblem of human existence, on the Greek legend of the mortal condemned for eternity to the futile and pointless task of pushing a boulder up an insurmountable peak. The vision of endless repetition of arduous, gratuitous labors is replicated in the structure, themes, and episodes of *The Plague*. *L'Homme révolté* (*The Rebel*) examines the individual's responsibility to defy a system felt to be oppressive. It was intended as Camus's major political testament, and its hostile reception proved his greatest disappointment as a writer and precipitated his notorious breach with Jean-Paul Sartre.

Of particular value in understanding the character of Tarrou in *The Plague* is Camus's polemic against capital punishment, "Réflexions sur la guillotine," an essay translated and collected in the volume *Resistance, Rebellion and Death*. On 11 January 1955, Camus sent a remarkable letter to critic Roland Barthes in which he analyzes *The Plague* as an allegory of World War II. The French text of the letter is available in volume 1 of the Pléiade Camus, and its English translation can be found in *Lyrical and Critical Essays*. Selections in that collection from *Noces* (*Nuptials*), *L'Été* (*Summer*), and *L'Envers et l'Endroit* (*The Right Side and the Wrong Side*) can provide students with some sense of the rhapsodic prose style that made *The Plague* a deliberate achievement in restraint and of the natural delight in the Algerian landscape that makes a gruesome epidemic in Oran so much more dismal.

Reference Works

The current volume swells the ocean of international Camus criticism, particularly in English. Assistance in surveying and navigating it all is provided by several bibliographies: Robert F. Roeming's *Camus: A Bibliography*; Francesco di Pilla's *Albert Camus e la critica: Bibliografia internazionale (1937–1971), con un saggio introduttivo*; and Raymond Gay-Crosier's "Albert Camus," in R. A. Brooks's *A Critical Bibliography of French Literature*. The annual *MLA International Bibliography* is an essential supplement to these works. Researchers should also consult the bibliographies published in the Camus annual edited by Brian T. Fitch for *La Revue des lettres modernes*.

Camus Studies

Some instructors, especially of lower-division and survey courses, discourage their students from reading any secondary materials, from displacing what should be the primary focus of attention: an unmediated encounter with *The Plague*. Others are grateful, on behalf of their students or themselves, for any of several books charting the Camus universe. These works include Germaine Brée, *Camus*; John Cruickshank, *Albert Camus and the Literature of Revolt*; Donald Lazere, *The Unique Creation of Albert Camus*; Albert Maquet, *Albert Camus: The Invincible Summer*; Roger Quilliot, *The Sea and Prisons*; and Philip Thody, *Albert Camus: A Study of His Work* and *Albert Camus 1913–1960*. Phillip H. Rhein's *Albert Camus* demonstrates the assets and liabilities of the Twayne format to which it conforms. Valuable collections of essays by divers hands on the entire Camus œuvre include Germaine Brée, ed., *Camus: A Collection of Critical Essays*; Raymond Gay-Crosier, ed., *Albert Camus, 1980*; and J. Lévi-Valensi, ed., *Albert Camus et les critiques de notre temps*. Some or all of them might well be placed on reserve to help orient the uninitiated student and to familiarize the more advanced one with the terms in which Camus scholarship is conducted.

Camus's very impersonality was distinctively personal, and students need some understanding of the position and function *The Plague* occupies within his career. The most thorough scholarly biography of the author likely to be published for a generation is Herbert R. Lottman's *Albert Camus: A Biography*. Patrick McCarthy's *Camus* is indebted to Lottman's research and aimed at a more general audience, including perhaps less advanced undergraduates. A very readable narrative, McCarthy's biography is especially strong on the North African coordinates of Camus's life and especially weak on literary analysis.

More specialized studies of Camus's days and works abound. Among book-length discussions are Fred H. Willhoite, Jr., *Beyond Nihilism: Albert Camus's Contribution to Political Thought*, and Jean Onimus, *Albert Camus and Christianity*. Conor Cruise O'Brien's *Albert Camus of Europe and Africa* argues that Camus was paralyzed as a writer and a political activist by his equivocation between Paris and Algiers, while in *Camus and Sartre: Crisis and Commitment*, Germaine Brée reexamines the dispute between Camus and Sartre and provides a spirited polemic in support of the former.

In La Peste: *Albert Camus*, Pol Gaillard devotes an entire volume to the novel of our concern, as does *Albert Camus 8*, the annual review of Camus studies edited by Brian T. Fitch for *La Revue des lettres modernes*; this number is entitled *Camus romancier:* La Peste. In *Albert Camus' The Plague: Introduction and Commentary by Thomas Merton*, the noted theologian examines the novel. And a Barron's guide to the book also exists: Donald Haggis, *Camus:* La Peste.

Bibliographies cite numerous recent articles that focus on themes and techniques of *The Plague*; of particular interest to students and their instructors are Robert W. Greene, "Fluency, Muteness and Commitment in Camus's *La Peste*"; Edwin P. Grobe, "Camus and the Parable of the Perfect Sentence"; Eugene Hollahan, "The Path of Sympathy: Abstraction and Imagination in Camus's *La Peste*"; Steven G. Kellman, "Singular Third Person: Camus' *La Peste*"; and Gerald J. Prince, "Le Discours attributif dans *La Peste*."

Background Studies

History

A sense of the course of twentieth-century French and North African history is as desirable as it is rare in students reading *The Plague* for the first time. Alfred Cobban, *A History of Modern France*, and Gordon Wright, *France in Modern Times*, provide magisterial overviews. The chapters—on history, philosophy, literature, contemporary society, and art and music—in *France: A Companion to French Studies*, edited by D. G. Charlton, have also been published as separate paperbacks. Herbert R. Lottman's *The Left Bank* examines the animated world of Parisian intellectuals in which Camus lived during and after World War II.

World War II is, according to Camus himself, the subtext of *The Plague*; and for most students, and many instructors, the Occupation and the Resistance will not even be distant memories. The history of Nazism is engagingly summarized for the general reader by William L. Shirer in *The Rise and Fall of the Third Reich*. Of the veritable industry of holocaust studies that has lately developed, Lucy S. Dawidowicz' *The War against the Jews* might be singled out for its comprehensiveness and scholarly rigor. Accounts of the French Resistance to Vichy and Berlin include Henri Michel, *Histoire de la Résistance en France*, and Philip P. Hallie, *Lest Innocent Blood Be Shed*. In a series of volumes—*Histoire de Vichy, Histoire de la libération*, and *Histoire de l'épuration*—the distinguished historian Robert Aron has examined the Vichy regime and its aftermath. A less monumental account, in English, is available in Robert O. Paxton, *Vichy France*. Konrad Bieber's *L'Allemagne vue par les écrivains de la Résistance* includes a preface by Camus himself. James D. Wilkinson's *The Intellectual Resistance in Europe* examines Camus among others.

It is not uncommon to discover that few, if any, American undergraduates in a lower-division class have even heard of the Algerian war, a major, gory trauma whose consequences are still palpable in the textures and tensions of French society. For a conscientious reader it is noteworthy that *The Plague* is set entirely in 1940s Algeria. Recent scholarship, having discovered the third world, emphasizes how very much, despite his habitation in Paris, Camus remained a North African by instinct. Alf Andrew Heggoy's *Historical Dictionary of Algeria* provides some sense of the forces shaping the world of *The Plague* and its *pied noir* author. And the following may be recommended as accounts of the Algerian war, which, though simmering for decades, did not erupt until after publication of *The Plague*: Henri Alleg, *La Guerre d'Algérie*; David C. Gordon, *The Passing of French Algeria*; and Jules Roy, *The War in Algeria*.

Literature

The place of *The Plague* in literary history may be explored through Jacques Bersani et al., *La Littérature en France depuis 1945*; Maurice Nadeau, *Le Roman français depuis la guerre*; and Henri Peyre, *French Novelists of Today*. The encyclopedic *Oxford Companion to French Literature*, edited by Paul Harvey and J. E. Heseltine, is appropriately titled and fruitfully consulted. *A History of French Literature*, by Louis François Cazamian, is a solid, generally reliable reference work.

The Novelist as Philosopher: Studies in French Fiction 1935–1960, edited by John Cruickshank, devotes an entire chapter to Camus and does a fine job of situating him in the company of other novelists of his time. Narrative technique is one of the fascinating elements in *The Plague*, and the undergraduate would do well to become familiar with Wayne C. Booth, *The Rhetoric of Fiction*, or Roland Bourneuf and Réal Ouellet, *L'Univers du roman* (1975), among many, many recent studies of fictional form. It was in reference to Camus's style that Roland Barthes coined the influential phrase "l'écriture blanche" 'white writing,' and Barthes's arguments in *Le Degré zéro de l'écriture* and *Essais critiques* on developments in French prose style enhance any reading of *The Plague*. Among the more remarkable developments since publication of *The Plague* has been the emergence of a movement calling itself *le nouveau roman*. In *Pour un nouveau roman*, Alain Robbe-Grillet, its most prominent practitioner, issues a manifesto calling for a kind of fiction that will transcend even the limpidity and impersonality that were Camus's ideals.

Philosophy

Many professional, especially analytical, philosophers are uncomfortable with the notion of Albert Camus as a colleague. Yet his career was fully consistent with the French tradition of *philosophe*, the man of letters who does not eschew ideas but directly addresses universal ethical issues. Two works that situate literature in general and Camus in particular within the categories of philosophical discourse are Everett W. Knight, *Literature Considered as Philosophy*, and Burton F. Porter, *Philosophy: A Literary and Conceptual Approach*.

Camus was and was not an existentialist, depending on how that elusive term is defined and how the equally elusive author is understood. Antecedents for many of Camus's essays and fictional conceits can be found in the writings of Kierkegaard, Nietzsche, Heidegger, Husserl, and Jaspers, and selections from them, as well as from such Camus associates as Sartre, Merleau-Ponty, and de Beauvoir, are conveniently collected in Robert C. Solomon, ed., *Existentialism*. Several absorbing studies of the existentialist movement and its claims have been written, including William Barrett, *Irrational Man*; Walter Kaufmann, *Existentialism from Dostoevsky to Sartre*; and William V. Spanos, ed., *Casebook on Existentialism Two*.

Sicknesses unto Death

As will be demonstrated by Ailene S. Goodman's essay in this volume, *The Plague* is part of a vibrant tradition of texts about epidemics. *The Plague* is frequently taught in a humanities course for medical students, and they and others might be curious about the realities of the disease dramatized in the novel. Recommended sources for information on the plague are Robert S. Gottfried, *The Black Death: Natural and Human Disaster in Medieval Europe*; L. Fabian Hirst, *The Conquest of Plague: A Study of the Evolution of Epidemiology*; William H. McNeill, *Plagues and People*; Johannes Nohl, *The Black Death*; Geddes Smith, *Plague on Us*; and Philip Ziegler, *The Black Death*. A quaint connection between epidemiology and modern French literature is *La Défense de l'Europe contre la peste*, by a prominent physician who was also Marcel Proust's father—Achille Adrien Proust. *The Plague* raises issues of medical ethics, and they are explored further in Earl Babbie, *Science and Morality in Medicine*; Richard G. Barton, *Death and Dying*; and H. Merskey and F. G. Spear, *Pain: Psychological and Physical Aspects*. In his imaginative response to the plague, Camus is in the illustrious company of the Bible, Sophocles, Boccaccio, Donne, Defoe, and Manzoni, among others. Useful discussions of disease as a literary theme include Raymond Crawfurd, *Plague and Pestilence in Literature and Art*; Ailene S. Goodman, "The Surgical Mask"; and Susan Sontag, *Illness as Metaphor*.

Audiovisual Aids

Most respondents to our survey were markedly apprehensive about using audio or visual materials to help teach a novel. Yet instructors ought at least to be aware of the possibilities, ranging from street maps of contemporary Oran to feature films.

Even nonfrancophonic students might be intrigued by the sound of Albert Camus's own voice, and it can be heard in a Caedmon recording, *Albert Camus Reading in French* (TC1138), released in 1960. On it, the author reads selections from *La Chute, La Peste, L'Etranger,* and *L'Eté. Albert Camus: A Self-Portrait*, produced by Fred Orjain, is a nineteen-minute film that, in black and white, shows Camus talking about the theater and then, in color, evokes the presence of Algeria. In twenty-one minutes, *Albert Camus*, a color filmstrip accompanied by a recording and produced by Thomas S. Klise, attempts to survey the author's career, while the fourteen-minute *Albert Camus*, produced by Judith Bantz, is similar in format and ambitions.

Only one of Camus's novels has been adapted for the cinema. In *L'Etranger*, director Luchino Visconti is obsequiously faithful to the text of Camus's first book. Credit for the screenplay of this version, starring Marcello Mastroianni and Anna Karina, is shared by Emmanuel Roblès, a friend of Camus's and himself a notable *pied noir* author, with Suso Cecchi d'Amico and Georges Conchon.

Although not explicitly Camusian, a screening of Gillo Pontecorvo's *La Battaglia di Algeri* might benefit students of *The Plague*. Without using one foot of actuality, the film manages to provide a graphic sense of documentary realism and to illuminate the forces that exploded in the Algerian revolution.

In 1950, only three years after publication of *The Plague, Panic in the Streets*, directed by Elia Kazan, was released. Set on the New Orleans waterfront, it is the story of a public-health official, played by Richard Widmark, intent on tracking down a murderer, played by Jack Palance, who is also thought to be carrying pneumonic plague. Of similar interest to students might be *Le Foulard de Smyrne*. Directed by François Villiers, with a screenplay by novelist Jean Giono, the film dramatizes an 1832 cholera epidemic in Provence.

Part Two

APPROACHES

INTRODUCTION

Germaine Brée, doyenne of Camus scholars and former president of the MLA, begins our series of essays with a personal review of Camus's career in North American academe. While more seasoned if no less salty, her account does not repudiate the judgment she published twenty-five years ago that "*La Peste* is, within its limits, a great novel, the most disturbing, most moving novel yet to have come out of the chaos of the mid-century." We are now closer to an equally chaotic fin du siècle, and some are more apt to dwell on this novel's limits than on its greatness. Yet, even without *les nouveaux philosophes'* belatedly canonizing Camus as a prophet of political moderation, he remains on this side of the Atlantic that rare phenomenon, a foreign writer widely read with genuine passion and affection, the most accessible of important French authors, whether read in English or skittish French.

The Plague is probably put to more versatile pedagogical use than most of the other texts examined in this MLA series. It is not the exclusive patent of French departments and is as likely to materialize in freshman composition classes, theological seminaries, and law schools as in literature courses. Hence, although instructors of modern French fiction clearly have a professional interest in how *The Plague* is taught, a deliberate effort was also made to involve other constituencies of the Modern Language Association, and indeed aliens—philosophers, theologians, political scientists, motley interdisciplinarians—as well. Most responded to our questionnaire with enthusiasm and generosity. The respondents represented a remarkable geographical, institutional, and disciplinary variety. Their approaches to apportionment of time, classroom discussion, assignments, and exams are so diverse as not to permit useful generalization. Instead, a subset of the larger group has been invited to speak for themselves in the following pages.

A comparatist, Konrad Bieber situates *The Plague* within the context of world literature, while Eva Van Ginneken, Jennifer Waelti-Walters, Irma M. Kashuba, and Eugenia N. Zimmerman outline approaches—through theme, structure, or theory—that can be presented to students of French. Current literary studies are manifestly neither monolithic nor, even of a text already as venerable as *La Peste*, paleolithic.

Camus's narrative is undeniably, and unfashionably, a novel of ideas, though on just what those ideas are intelligent men and women differ. Its concern with ethical, political, and legal issues—like capital punishment, theodicy, resistance, and euthanasia—makes it effective in the kinds of courses that Richard T. Lambert, Robert R. Brock, and Ailene S. Goodman teach.

And it should be self-evident that a novel set in Algeria with allusions to the Nazi Occupation and written in French by a native of North Africa cannot be understood *in vacuo*, or in a North American classroom devoid of background materials. The essays by Allen Thiher, Martha O'Nan, and Catharine Savage Brosman provide the instructor with historical, biographical, and geographical coordinates for reading the novel, at the same time as they demonstrate how these elements can be effective in presenting the work in an academic setting.

Our valedictorian, Mary Ann Caws, is another prominent scholar of modern French literature and former president of the Modern Language Association. A class, an essay, or a book on *The Plague* may come to a halt; but the text itself bides its time in bedrooms, cellars, trunks, and bookshelves, ready to become again the bane and enlightenment of readers, scholars, teachers, and students.

PROLOGUE
Germaine Brée

"If you had read the *Parti-Pris*, without knowing me *at all*, do you think you would have thought it important? . . . If your answer is affirmative, then I feel no obligation to furnish any further explanation" (qtd. in Lottman 292, French ed.; trans mine).[1] So, in 1943, wrote Francis Ponge—then a little-known poet—to his young friend Albert Camus, whom the double publication, in 1942, of *The Stranger* and *The Myth of Sisyphus* was rapidly making famous. Ponge's question and answer concern us here. A quarter of a century after Camus's death, will those who did not "know" Camus consider *The Plague* if not "important"—a somewhat unsatisfactory term—at least worth reading? Clearly the contributors to this volume think it is, but, as the title suggests, their purpose is not to "explain" but to present different "approaches," different ways of relating to the text. *The Plague* is a challenging book because it has had a paradoxical career in France, showing "a singular adventure in our [French] culture" (André Abbou, in Gay-Crosier, *Camus, 1980* 277). French critics have been reticent about *The Plague*. But readers have not followed suit. The first edition of 22,000 copies—an optimistic estimate, it was thought, of the book's appeal—was rapidly sold out. In the next four months, sales had risen to more than 100,000 copies. In 1980, *The Plague* was still high on the list of literary best-sellers. It had sold 3,700,000 copies. Furthermore, it had reached a worldwide reading public; translations appeared in eleven languages, and any fairly complete bibliography of critical and scholarly studies of *The Plague* points to its continuing "importance" in literary studies.[2]

It would be impossible to give an adequate account of the various approaches to the text. From the vantage point of the eighties, we can see that its first readers understood it in the context of their own historical situation, the experience of the war years and the German Occupation—and in a limited way they were right to do so. They brought to their critical evaluations of Camus's book the political passions of the hour or their personal ideological points of view. For example, the young Roland Barthes, in a letter to Camus that was mostly appreciative, reproached Camus for having evaded the problem of violence by pitting the citizens of Oran against a faceless enemy and so bypassing the question of right and wrong. Camus, he felt, had avoided corroborating the judgment of history. It was a criticism often to be reiterated and was charged with political implications. The hope of the future for many intellectuals at the end of the war lay in establishing a truly "just" socialist state: modeled along the Russian pattern, a utopian view of an idealized political reality. Camus, who was always to remain a socialist, had been a member of the Communist party in his Algerian youth but had been expelled for his refusal to accept the policies dictated by Moscow. He did not share the orthodox neo-Marxist view of history, class conflict, and the necessary march of humanity powered by the proletariat toward the classless society, which automatically placed people according to their political affiliation to the "right" or the "wrong" side of history.

Another trend among critics has been to base an interpretation of *The Plague* on an "existentialist" ideology that Camus never shared. More pertinently, *The Plague* was read in the light of Camus's previous essay defining what he called "the absurd," that is, in a secular context, the thinking person's confrontation with the incomprehensible: death, suffering, the longing for absolutes, the evidence of unavoidable contradictions and relativity. That the confrontation with the plague is a confrontation with the incomprehensible, even with the unimaginable, is true. But it is not an abstract confrontation. Most of the plague's victims suffer its effects dumbly, physically unable to conceptualize the nightmare in which they are plunged. One cannot reduce *The Plague* to an abstract model, nor can one build an interpretation on the assumption that the plague itself "stands for" some specific evil, though evil in human terms it certainly is.

The very choice of the plague as the dynamic ordering force of the book tempts us into making a quick interpretation, into moving rapidly from the surface of the text to its "message." Thence the frequent statement that *The Plague* is not a novel but a moral allegory seems flawed. Whether or not it is a novel is a matter for definition: what definition of a novel is being used as a criterion? and what definition of allegory? There are many kinds of novels and many levels of allegory.

Other critics have approached the text as narrative fiction, defining its strategies and structure: who tells the story? is his the only point of view through which all others are refracted? how does the narrative progress? why are there five parts? is there such a thing as a "plot"? if so, what is plotted? what is the function of the dialogues? of the descriptive passages? of the choice of the city, Oran, deliberately on the periphery of the war zone? and of the principal characters? Closely linked to this approach are other questions: What does the *language* tell us about the characters, Rieux's for instance, as opposed to Paneloux's, the doctor's as opposed to the priest's? What does it convey to the reader? How do the changing descriptions of Oran during the invasion of the plague affect the reader's attitude toward the citizens of Oran? Are there discrepancies that disconcert or puzzle or that open discontinuities in the texture of the narrative?

Many critics, as time passed, have wished to situate *The Plague* in regard not only to previous works—*The Stranger, The Myth of Sisyphus*, and the two plays *Caligula* and *The Misunderstanding*—but also to subsequent works. Camus himself in his notebooks suggested such an ordering, positing a deliberate logical progression in stages. In this context *The Plague* appears as the first step in moving beyond the boundaries of the "absurd," or rather, perhaps, working within those boundaries to explore the power of human beings to make human sense of their lot even in the most stringent circumstances. Prometheus, the Titan who, rebelling against Zeus, stole fire to bring its civilizing power to humankind, is the mythic guide to this second phase, as Sisyphus, a rebel too, is a guide to the first.[3] The principal characters in *The Plague* with the exception of one, Dr. Rieux's mother, rebel against the inhuman order infused by the plague. But how about that serene mother figure? Furthermore, if we stop to think about the word itself— "plague"—Camus leaves us no doubt from the first page that it designates the real bubonic plague. But in English we often talk about what "plagues" us, and all the characters except Mme Rieux, we are told, are "plagued"— by what? We also talk about pests, whether invading destructive insects and rodents or annoying people, nuisances. In French, *la peste* almost always designates the epidemic disease, but *une peste* can in either anger or amusement designate a person, as in English. Where we say a "plague of locusts," for instance, the French would use *invasion*. *Pester* in French means to rage against something, a more virulent sense than "to pester"; and *empester* means to stink obtrusively, as the city of Oran stinks from the fumes of the cremation pits. Something about Camus's city as we reach the center of the book smacks of hell, a temporary descent into hell. Thence, as in Dante, there is an emergence from the inferno. In Camus's secular world, that emergence is accompanied by a fresh love of the world: the bells ring; the sun shines; fireworks illuminate the sky; the crowd shouts its relief and joy. Earth once again is a familiar earth, a good earth. The two vistas do not cancel each other out, as Dr. Rieux knows.

Since Camus's death in 1960, many previously unpublished texts have come out, several that throw light on the slow genesis of *The Plague*. It took Camus some seven years to write the text and to contrive its structure. In 1943 a first draft was finished and discarded. Herbert Lottman's fully doc- umented biography of Camus describes the personal circumstances in which Camus lived during the dismal years of the Occupation. "Plagued" by tu- berculosis, he was advised by his doctors to rest in a quiet mountain village. Very hard up, he chose a small bleak village in the Cevennes mountains, in unoccupied France. He was about to join his wife and family in Algiers when the Allied landing in North Africa and the consequent total occupation of France by the Germans left him in a kind of complete isolation. Many notes and some letters record his desperate struggle not to give way to despair. Slowly he emerged from his solitude and illness, making friends among the village men, some of whom, unknown to him at the time, were working with resistance groups. He hardly knew that his two books—*The Stranger* and *The Myth of Sisyphus*—had come out. But at the end of 1943 he was on his way to Paris to a paid job as reader for the Gallimard editions and to active involvement in the clandestine press. Almost overnight, he found himself at the hub of the French literary world, and he was soon one of its celebrities. Camus was thirty. It would take another three years before *The Plague* was ready to come out. Hard though these years were, they were the years of freedom recovered. The explosion of joy expressed by the citizens of Oran, as the plague moves away and returns them to the open world of human contacts and projects, echoes the delirious joy of the Parisians at the liberation of their city in August 1944. *The Plague* was indeed influ- enced by a personally experienced collective set of events.

But that is not all. Camus's notebooks tell us what in those years Camus read, the enormous and meticulous research that underlies the deliberately told account of Dr. Rieux. But one book is particularly of interest because it has nothing to do with Camus's central image: Melville's *Moby-Dick*, which Camus read in a recent French translation. At first sight the vast horizon and turbulence of Melville's novel seem the very opposite of the closed city of the plague-stricken citizens of Oran. If I may be allowed to end on a personal note, I remember vividly the day when Camus explained to me how greatly he admired not only Melville's handling of the literal setting of the whaling expedition but also the different levels of signification suggested by Captain Ahab's obsessive pursuit of the white whale. But he felt that the great horizons and mystery of the ocean, the towering figure of the protag- onist were closely linked to the Romantic sensibility and imagination. The

claustrophobic world of war, prison, concentration camp, and torture required the creation of a different kind of space, the closing in of stifling
constraints. This is the level at which a reader may most personally sense
the integrative force that holds together all the facets of *The Plague*.

NOTES

[1] *Le Parti-Pris des choses* is the title of a small volume of prose poems in which
Ponge broke with the highly intellectual tradition of poetry, exemplified by Mallarmé,
and "took the side of things." He carefully described the familiar objects we take for
granted: a cigarette, the telephone—an approach that appealed to Camus.

[2] I am indebted to Ilona Coombs, who drew these figures to my attention.

[3] For a full and remarkably rich discussion of the Promethean myth and its relation
to Camus's work, see *Albert Camus: The Essential Writings* 111–229.

THE PLAGUE AS WORLD LITERATURE

Meaning and Message in *The Plague*

Konrad Bieber

How much is there to "teach" when novels are assigned to young readers? To be sure, a firm method is to be followed consistently if the reader is to perceive the book's message, provided there is one. Since single-book assignments are rare except in seminar work, there will be comparisons for the student to consider. Thus, if eight to ten novels are to be read over the course of a semester, naturally personal preferences will be voiced and are, I believe, to be welcomed. My experience has been that when American writers are read alongside authors from less familiar continents, students will prefer the Americans. Thus Steinbeck's *The Grapes of Wrath*, read in two classes of thirty-five students each, five years apart, was far and away the first choice. One of the classes rated Malraux's *Man's Fate* a close second, while a more recent group put Malraux last of ten authors and Camus second. Camus's *The Plague* had ranked third five years earlier in a course that also used Voltaire's *Candide*, Ellison's *Invisible Man* (recently a very close competitor with Camus), Heinrich Böll's *Billiards at Half Past Nine*, Arthur Koestler's *Darkness at Noon*, Ray Bradbury's *Fahrenheit 451*, Max Frisch's *Andorra*, and Jean-Paul Sartre's plays *No Exit*, *The Flies*, and *Dirty Hands*.

Popularity alone should not necessarily decide the choice of a book to be studied closely. But students like novels in which they can identify or empathize to some extent with the protagonists and their motives. How else measure the appeal of texts? This affinity seems to me particularly important in the light of the marked changes that tend to take place from one student generation to the next. Such changes are not of course a purely American phenomenon; reports from other countries indicate strong shifts in readers' allegiance every five years or even more frequently.

In a typical fourteen-week semester, students given assignments on Camus's *The Plague* raise a number of challenging questions. First, many wonder why there has to be a plague. Aren't plagues a thing of the past? And even if they did exist once do they have any bearing on our age? Granted that the novel is an allegory, couldn't the author have chosen another way of expressing his idea?

In attempting to answer some of these questions, one has to use the text itself to dispel misunderstandings or misreadings. The book's epigraph, for instance, helps explain why Camus chose a plague: representing one thing through another, the author confronts the reader with a reality strong enough to infuse the work with the breath of life. Different interpretations of that reality may be legitimate; yet the reading that prevails over any other, as will appear from the quotation below, is that human beings must resist evil and death.

Apprised of Camus's earlier fascination with "the absurd," students are quick to point to several themes and recurring episodes in *The Plague* that mirror this preoccupation: the old man who from his balcony lured cats to his stoop only to spit on them; the old Spaniard, an asthma patient of Dr. Rieux, who spent his days endlessly counting chick-peas from one pot into another; the literary ambitions of Grand, the clerk, culminating in his one-sentence opening scene for a novel never to be completed. Speaking of the importance of "the absurd" in Camus's early life and work, one should not fail to evoke his tragic death, further illustration of the fateful irony presiding over his life.

Questioned on more substantial points, on values and ideas transcending the immediate action, students are prompt in mentioning friendship as one positive element in *The Plague*. Solidarity, the simple quality of involvement for the benefit of others, is an obvious part of Camus's story. The fight against evil and illness and ultimately the protest against any form of "separation" and death are motives that strike young readers if they direct their attention to essentials. A more sophisticated reading from a linguistic point of view, done by a graduate research assistant in 1982, produced hundreds of terms used by the author, all connected with the idea of separation—a study far too specialized to use in a college classroom but fitting for a graduate group.

Likewise, Gerald J. Prince has provided an excellent study of some of Camus's stylistic idiosyncrasies, again on a level not readily usable, except in its conclusions, for undergraduate teaching. In Prince's judgment, Camus makes a deliberate effort to dedramatize, to avoid picturesque description in order to concentrate on fundamentals.

If students ask the instructor what exactly the allegory attempts to portray, a political or historical explanation is nothing to eschew. Even though Camus's ambition may have far exceeded an evocation of France during World War II, a more abstract vision of humanity's struggle for freedom and independence or an aspiration toward higher goals constitutes a fitting interpretation of *The Plague* and satisfies the thirst for knowledge. In this connection, a discussion of Camus's models could prove helpful. Besides Roger Martin du Gard, whose example Camus hailed, and Dostoevsky, who may have inspired certain moods and a few of the characters, there is a strong dose of Kafka to be noted throughout *The Plague*. The withholding of the narrator's identity until the end of the book, the avoidance of precise details in the descriptions of most events, the speech patterns, and in general the detachment with which the narrative unfolds—all these clearly point to Kafka as a major influence. A few years ago an undergraduate literature class read *The Plague* along with Kafka's *The Castle* and some German and Italian novels also in some fashion imbued with Kafka's example. Students readily detected a strong influence on Camus, although they found equal evidence of Kafkaesque elements in others, especially the German writers.

Students may be referred to secondary sources if the level of their readings justifies such research. Germaine Brée's *Camus*, John Cruickshank's *Albert Camus and the Literature of Revolt*, and Philip Thody's *Albert Camus: A Study of His Work* are still clearly the best, since normally students cannot be expected to plow through the formidable and very competent and complete biography by Herbert Lottman or the more esoteric discussions of Camus's work. The most recent critical study of Camus, by Patrick McCarthy, is disappointing. It may be a good and reliable source for Camus's political background, his early flirtation with communism, his leadership in the theatrical group, and the general conditions in North Africa. It is, however, an utter misreading of the literary work, particularly *The Plague*. When I read relevant passages from McCarthy's book to my students, without identifying the author, the strange statement "the patients hate Rieux because he cannot cure them" (228), was greeted with an explosion of laughter. Similarly, McCarthy's overemphasis on religious ideas in the mature Camus is dangerously wrong and misleading; critics bent on a well-reasoned analysis of Camus's expressed ideas make short shrift of such extravagant readings.

Reference to Camus's life is in order if it serves to enliven the discussion and explain major ideas in the novel. I found it valuable to evoke briefly Camus's role in the Resistance—a role, incidentally, that McCarthy slights, without any foundation. Several episodes in *The Plague* gain clarity through such historicobiographical explanations. Indeed, Camus's nebulous references to the "authorities" could be an allusion to Kafka, but circumstantial evidence suggests that the picture fits the years of Nazi Occupation and the Vichy government far better and more concretely. It is only fair to remind students that, naturally, Camus was far from being the only writer depicting the political atmosphere in France between 1940 and 1944; even during the Occupation, Sartre, in *The Flies*, and Jean Anouilh, in *Antigone*, hardly veiled their barbs against both the Vichy collaborators and the Germans. Students may have read both plays. In Anouilh's *Antigone* we see the closest parallel to the situation that prevails in *The Plague*. Despite Créon's plea that one must submit, Antigone maintains that one's first duty as a human being is to act in accordance with one's conscience. The same message is clearly expressed in *The Plague*. For brevity's sake, I will quote only the most essential sentences in a long and beautiful passage. They are from Stuart Gilbert's translation, which, with a few flaws, most adequately renders the text:

> These groups enabled our townsfolk to come to grips with the disease and convinced them that, now that plague was among us, it was up to them to do whatever could be done to fight it. Since plague became in this way some men's duty, it revealed itself as what it really was; that is, the concern of all.
>
> So far, so good. But we do not congratulate a schoolmaster on teaching that two and two make four. . . . it was praiseworthy that Tarrou and so many others should have elected to prove that two and two make four rather than the contrary; but let us add that this good will of theirs was one that is shared by the schoolmaster and by all who have the same feelings as the schoolmaster, and, be it said to the credit of mankind, they are more numerous than one would think—such, anyhow, is the narrator's conviction. Needless to say, he can see quite clearly a point that could be made against him, which is that these men were risking their lives. But again and again there comes a time in history when the man who dares to say that two and two make four is punished with death. The schoolteacher is well aware of this. And the question is not one of knowing what punishment or reward attends the making of this calculation. The question is that of knowing whether two and two do make four. For those of our townsfolk who risked their lives in this predicament the issue was whether or not the plague was in their midst and whether or not they must fight against it.   (Mod. Lib. Coll. ed. 121–22)

This significant text found a new and tragic illustration in a cartoon published, surprisingly, in Czechoslovakia in recent years. A little man carries a banner modestly saying "2 × 2 = 4," while huge wall posters and airplane fliers proclaim everywhere "2 × 2 = 5." Students who have read *The Plague* need no further explanation.

The long quotation needs a conclusion, though, in the even more explicit and topical paragraph immediately after the one quoted:

> Many fledgling moralists in those days were going about our town proclaiming there was nothing to be done about it and we should bow to the inevitable. And Tarrou, Rieux, and their friends might give one answer or another, but its conclusion was always the same, their certitude that a fight must be put up, in this way or that, and there must be no bowing down. The essential thing was to save the greatest possible number of persons from dying and being doomed to unending separation. And to do this there was only one resource: to fight the plague. There was nothing admirable about this attitude, it was merely logical.   (122)

Biographical and historical elements also help orient students toward a more exact evaluation of the role of nature, particularly the sea, in Camus's work in general and in *The Plague* specifically. Nature, in fact, provides a fine key for recognizing Rieux's and Tarrou's source of strength. More than a mere escape from drudgery and a depressing environment, the sea acts as a tonic on both men, and the harmony between them is reinforced through the sharing of a delight in bodily exercise, sunshine, and temporary serenity. Advanced students may also be referred to Roger Quilliot's book *The Sea and Prisons*.

If maintaining solidarity, obstinately opposing evil and death, and caring for and healing the plague-stricken are easily understood and accepted by students, the seemingly pessimistic conclusion of the novel may be resisted by some. Since the plague is finally conquered, or simply subsides as suddenly as it came, why the sober yet emphatic statement suggesting the likelihood that the evil will recur? There is no easy answer to this question, nor is there, in my view, an entirely satisfactory one, except, perhaps, to say that Camus did not want a simple "happy ending" to this tale of life and death, of humanity's never-ending struggle with nature, with death.

The ending is in line with much of Camus's thought as it appears throughout his writing—in his fiction and his plays, with their frankly pessimistic outlook on life but also their rebellion against seemingly insurmountable odds. But in *The Plague* readers will perceive that a return of the plague would once more call forth the human response of resistance. Again, there would be a struggle, a mobilization of goodwill and devotion to the stricken, a forceful show of solidarity.

Camus's essays emphasize the same kind of pessimism. It is akin to that

of Voltaire or Sartre—who are so different from Camus in most other respects. Camus's use of humor is like theirs too. Even in the tragic events
recounted in *The Plague*, there is often an undertone of irony. His deft sense
of humor not only shows up in the description of Grand and his futile pursuits
but permeates the whole novel with a quiet tone of slight amusement.
Alongside stern considerations on death and life are countless examples of
a more sanguine view, of compassionate yet occasionally condescending
remarks.

The pessimism of Voltaire, of Sartre, of Camus, and of many writers ever
since Montaigne's day stems from an activist view of the individual's task in
this world. Where Voltaire mocked the passive, indolent attitude of the
optimist and preached combat against war, superstition, ignorance, and big-
otry, Sartre, like Anatole France, took up the good fight in this century.
Activism need not take the more naive form of the street demonstrations
Sartre loved. In Camus, action and word combine to convey a message of
conscience to the world. Camus remains a humanist whose pessimism does
not detract from his example as a healer in a universe still in search of
meaning and much in need of a guiding light.

TEACHING *LA PESTE* IN FRENCH LITERATURE COURSES

Conquering the Plague

Eva Van Ginneken

In response to student complaints during the late 1960s that the reading material required for the French major was "irrelevant," my colleagues and I set about reexamining and, eventually, revising our undergraduate program. We decided to replace our traditional survey courses, in which equal time and attention had been allotted to every period from the Middle Ages to the present, by a series of new courses emphasizing the high points of French civilization and especially the modern era. We now combine the study of the Middle Ages and Renaissance in one course, devote one each to classicism and romanticism and four senior seminars to the twentieth century. Although the last four are "theme" courses, each tends to cover a particular movement or moment of contemporary civilization. The works read, however, are not necessarily restricted to that moment. For example, the first course in the series, called Exploration of the Self (475A), deals primarily with the work of the generation of Gide, Proust, and Mauriac but also includes Camus's *La Chute*. The other courses are 475B—In Search of the Real (surrealism), 475C—The Individual and Society (existentialism), and 475D—Beyond Despair (postexistentialist literature). *The Plague (La Peste)* is taught in 475C.

La Peste is one of four or five texts that, except for two handouts, compose the entire reading list. More is not asked because the course is taught in French and the works must be read in the original. (The handouts, one an outline by dates of the development of commercial aviation in France, the other, also by dates, of European penetration of China at the end of the nineteenth century, are brief and to the point. Their sole purpose is to furnish the students with a historical background and political context for the reading of Saint-Exupéry and Malraux.) Although a course in literary analysis and at least two other French literature courses are prerequisites to this seminar, the language continues to present problems to some, even at this stage, and the content may, at first, seem unfamiliar to many. It therefore seems preferable to limit the amount of material to be tackled and to ask the students to read the amount assigned slowly and carefully. For the same reason, recourse to secondary sources is discouraged. Many times, undergraduates do not understand that secondary sources are works of interpretation, characterized by value judgments, which must themselves be read critically. In fact, experience has taught me that one of the major problems students encounter in writing and evaluating their own papers is the notion that, although there is usually no single "correct" answer to the questions that a work of literature may raise, some answers are, nevertheless, more valid and useful than others. Time, of course, would not permit rereading and reexamining the works assigned several times, in the light of various critical opinions. But the most important consideration here is that it is a direct and *personal* response to the work that I mean to encourage.

The authors always included in this seminar are Saint-Exupéry, Malraux, Sartre, and Camus. By Saint-Exupéry, the students read *Terre des hommes* or *Vol de nuit*; by Malraux, *La Condition humaine*; by Sartre at least one of the following titles: *Huis-Clos*, *Les Mains sales*, *Morts sans sépulture*, *Les Mouches*, and "L'Enfance d'un chef" from the collection *Le Mur*; by Camus always *La Peste*. Students are encouraged to take Exploration of the Self (475A) before they take 475C. Most of them do so. Since the first course deals with the quest for self-knowledge and the search for identity as individual and as artist, it provides the student with an invaluable background to the study of existentialism. On those occasions when most students have not taken 475A, I like to begin 475C with a work by Gide. I believe that the one best suited to the theme and objectives of this course is *Les Faux-Monnayeurs*, but, because of its length, which impinges too much on the time that can be allotted to the other books, I tend to use either *La Symphonie pastorale*, *L'Immoraliste*, or *La Porte étroite*.

The organization of the course is determined not only by the number of works studied and the number of weeks available but also by the difficulty of the texts, the background of the students, and their reactions to the material. There is, therefore, a certain degree of flexibility in the reading schedule. The dates indicated on the syllabus are tentative. The first week, which I consider one of the most important of the semester, is spent in a general discussion of the themes that will occupy us. When only four authors are read, the remaining time of a fifteen-week semester (three hours a week) is divided as follows: two weeks of class discussion are devoted to Saint-Exupéry, four to Malraux, four to Sartre (two are spent on one of the plays and two on "L'Enfance d'un chef"), and four to Camus. When Gide is added to the program, two weeks are devoted to one of his novels and three each to Malraux and Camus. The students are asked to read ahead and to make every effort to finish each work before its discussion in class begins. There are three reasons for that insistence. The first is to avoid misinterpretation of individual passages considered out of context, the second to ensure that each student is prepared to participate in class discussions, and the third to allow students time for writing their papers without falling behind in the reading. They write three or four papers. Some papers deal with a single work, but most require students to compare the treatment of a major theme by two authors. The assignments are four to five pages long and might have subjects such as: "Compare the treatment of one of the following themes in Malraux and Saint-Exupéry: dignity, fraternity, responsibility" or "Discuss the problem of happiness in *La Peste.*" There are no formal examinations, and the final grade is based on the written analyses and on class participation. The main objective of the course is to lead the students to an understanding both of some of the basic concepts of existentialist thinking and of the intellectual climate of France at midcentury.

The discussions of the first week are designed to establish a method and especially to set the tone, which will be personal, for the rest of the semester. I think it important to get the students involved as quickly as possible in the problems they are about to encounter in the literature. A personal tone and a constant exchanging of ideas and sharing of reactions help to convince students that these problems are of immediate interest. Each student must be permitted, indeed compelled, at the very beginning, to "situate" himself or herself in a group (of classmates) as well as in relation to the instructor and to become accustomed to the tenor of thinking of the authors. While it is rarely possible to get students to forget that the instructor is in a different position (this is a class, after all, and however exciting the discussion may become, grades are hard to forget), my aim is to move as far as possible beyond the usual polite "rapport" we try to establish with students. "Situating" ourselves should come closer to the Sartrian meaning of "*situation.*" It should convey the feeling of Pascal's "Nous sommes embarqués." To the extent that this effort succeeds, the students will perceive both the situations in which the characters find themselves and their reactions to these situations as "real" and relevant. They will come to feel that these matters concern us all.

To facilitate the process just described, the discussions during the first few meetings tend to be general and unstructured, just as the first reading assignment is the least demanding, both linguistically and philosophically (Gide or Saint-Exupéry). Later, as the analysis and interpretation of the works in question begin to take precedence over immediate, subjective response, more discipline is required. Personal reactions, however, continue to be taken into account, both to sustain lively interest and to keep the method inductive throughout. The books are not to be read as illustrations or embodiments of principles; rather, each work is treated as an autonomous whole, then related and compared to the ones previously read. Ideally, these comparisons develop, by the end of the semester, an ability to recognize and identify common preoccupations and many shared attitudes among the authors. Abstract theories are also avoided at the beginning of the semester and kept to a minimum later. Given the works' themes—human dignity, solitude, fraternity, and, especially, the problem of personal freedom as opposed to the existential sense of responsibility toward one's fellows—it is possible to involve every student in our topic from the start. I often start very informally, by referring to some recent newspaper or magazine article, a television program, or a campus event. These items might deal with anything from a proposed increase in tuition fees to espionage for one's country or for the enemy to starvation in a refugee camp or among a certain tribe to murder. As the students voice their opinions, as comments and disagreements are expressed, frames of reference are built for later use. It is usually possible, regardless of the opinions held, to lead the class to realize that, while using a different vocabulary, they had been debating about values and choices relating to our themes: dignity and humiliation, fraternity and solitude, freedom and responsibility. These initial informal conversations have the incidental but important benefit of giving me the opportunity to evaluate students' linguistic proficiencies, to familiarize myself with their various backgrounds in literature and philosophy, and thereby to anticipate some of the problems individual students might encounter in the course of the semester.

After the first or second meeting, I present to the class, in the form of quotations or explanations, points of view by earlier authors that run counter to existentialist tenets. The ones I have found most useful are Jules Romain's concept of "*unanimisme*" and Romain Rolland's advocacy of taking a position "*au-dessus de la mêlée.*" To this material I add one or more short passages by Sartre dealing with the notion of "*engagement*," such as: "Si tout homme est embarqué cela ne veut point dire qu'il en ait pleine conscience; la plupart passent leur temps à se dissimuler leur engagement" (123–24). Or, "Je dirai qu'un écrivain est engagé lorsqu'il tâche à prendre la conscience la plus lucide et la plus entière d'être embarqué, c'est-à-dire lorsqu'il fait passer pour lui et pour les autres l'engagement de la spontanéité immédiate au réfléchi" (124). There are several advantages to this procedure. First, a note of objectivity is introduced into the discussion since we must now begin to deal with a text or at least someone else's opinion. Second, the juxtaposition of such divergent attitudes not only clarifies but seems to intensify the student's comprehension of all that *engagement* implies. Third, a comparison of the dates at which these ideas were formulated calls the student's attention to the connection between radical changes in thinking and the historical events that were taking place at the same time. Finally, the material helps students understand that there is more than one "respectable" stance they might adopt in life and that, although the existentialist point of view is, of necessity, emphasized in the course, they are not being compelled to accept it. (It often happens that in "theme" courses, which by their nature are "one-sided," undergraduates consider their errors of interpretation as "disagreements" and sometimes look on correction as punishment for holding a different point of view.)

Any of the novels mentioned above by Gide and Saint-Exupéry can be a good lead-in to the works that follow. They serve as a useful transition from a body of traditional literature set in a stable world order to a universe in which the individual stands alone. Students can observe in Gide's work characters who not only believe in God but who dedicate or sacrifice their (worldly) life to him, even while behaving, despite their beliefs, in ways that are morally reprehensible or at the very least ambiguous. They learn here the supreme importance of sincerity—or, as the later term has it, "authenticity"—with oneself and others; in its absence truly moral choices are impossible. Gide's characters face many of the problems that result from an evolution of spiritual values, just as Saint-Exupéry's characters must confront the challenges created by a rapidly developing technology. In the same way, Malraux's protagonists must keep rebuilding their lives, begin new lives, or give up their lives, as they find themselves in constantly changing circumstances caused by political upheavals. All live in a world being transformed by forces no individual can control. Nevertheless, each person must attempt to influence the direction of these forces, and each must do it alone. Work may be done with and for others, but every choice must be made alone. The class progresses through a series of works in which God is first an ambivalent presence, then absent, and finally denied. I find that by the time the discussions of Gide, Saint-Exupéry, and Malraux's *La Condition humaine* are over, and sometimes long before, everyone has understood that, regardless of personal belief, the themes and ideas under consideration must be evaluated in an atheistic context and that such terms as "solitude" and "fraternity," "liberty," and "anguish" (*angoisse*) have acquired an appropriate metaphysical weight. "Solitude" no longer describes being alone on Saturday night or "anguish" feeling apprehensive about an upcoming test. At this point, I find it useful to summarize the concepts dealt with so far. A summary solidifies the existentialist ground on which we now stand. It has become easy to understand, even obvious, why, in an ever-changing, ever more complex world, devoid of moral absolutes and divine guidance, the search for an ethic is these authors' main concern.

In the works studied so far, many questions have been raised and examples of possible lines of conduct given. With Sartre, we are ready to examine some paradoxes. I use one of the plays to make clear both the difficulty and the necessity of reconciling such apparently contradictory concepts as "*situation*" and "liberty," "liberty" and "*engagement.*" In *Les Mouches*, for example, the willingness or refusal to accept responsibility for one's actions and the consequences of each choice can be studied both by examining the statements and choices made by the protagonist, Oreste, and by comparing his behavior with that of Electre and with that of the other citizens of Argos. In each of the works we read in this course, the most insistent theme points to the impact that one individual's actions can have on others; the actions include submission to discipline in Saint-Exupéry, the struggle of the revolutionaries in Malraux, assassination in *Les Mouches* and, of course, fighting the plague in Camus. What is more strongly conveyed in Sartre and Camus than in the others is the conviction that making conscious choices, choices with the rest of humanity in mind, is a moral imperative. Choices must be made despite uncertainty, and struggles must be carried on despite certain failure, despite the "*Absurd.*" It is while working with the texts by Sartre that I introduce a few technical terms and abstract concepts such as Sartre's "*projet existentiel*" and Camus's idea of the "*Absurd.*" (Although at this point I usually inform the class of Camus's protestations that he was not an existentialist, I don't pursue the subject. I don't believe that his differences with Sartre are relevant to an investigation of the intellectual kinship among several authors or that the technical designation is important to our topic.)

One of the most difficult tasks is dealing with many students' perception of this literature as "negative" and "pessimistic." It is necessary to keep reminding them of the historical and political circumstances at the time of writing and to explain that the settings are sinister and the tone pessimistic precisely to the extent that the works measure up to what Sartre called their "*historicité.*" The remarkable phenomenon that must be repeatedly emphasized is that, even in these circumstances, human beings are capable of being dignified (like the pilots in Saint-Exupéry), noble (like Kyo and especially Katow in *La Condition humaine*), and even godlike (like Oreste in

Les Mouches). For some, however, empathy with these characters is difficult, perhaps because the heroic deeds are few. From the perspective of a total moral code, the characters' responses are sometimes fragmentary (Oreste's one irremediable act) and sometimes in fact negative, like a character's demonstrating what not to do, how not to think (Lucien in "L'Enfance d'un chef"), the proper course of action having to be inferred. *La Peste*, by contrast, is perceived by most students as "positive." What is more, the setting, the characters, and the circumstances in which they find themselves seem "normal" to students. One may ask how the life of a town living in what is essentially a state of siege can appear normal. I think several factors account for this reaction. It seems easier for students to respond to illness and disease as reality and as metaphor than to the harsh conditions characteristic of the preceding works, typical of what Sartre called a *"littérature de grandes circonstances."* The latter demand heroic responses and grandiose gestures of which few are capable. *La Peste* stresses the ordinary from the first paragraph. We hear what happens in an ordinary town whose ordinary citizens lead ordinary lives. Even the events of the plague are described as only "somewhat" unusual. The understated style and quiet tone of the narration, the modesty of the protagonists, the interest and respect shown for everyday ("normal") preoccupations, such as how to escape or cure disease, how to fulfill one's duties as a human being and citizen, how to find happiness—all communicate more effectively the conviction that everyone is involved in the drama that is the plague.

By the time students read *La Peste*, the assimilation of the main tenets of existentialist thinking and of the major themes of existentialist literature has prepared them to accept immediately the setting of the story and to live the events of the epidemic with the characters. But, conversely, I often feel the need, at this point, to prevent students from being misled by the deceptive simplicity of the style and by the dreary atmosphere into believing that the characters function only on an everyday rather than on a philosophical level. To show that we are still dealing with the same concerns and the same dilemmas, I begin the discussion of the book closer to the end than to the beginning. As soon as answers have been given to some standard opening questions (Who is (are) the main character(s)? Who is telling the story? To whom? Why?), I ask the class "What is the plague?" Usually, several suggestions are put forth: illness, falsehood, life, death, evil. I do not reject any of these readings and mention in passing the German Occupation of France during World War II, which rarely comes up otherwise. I point out that more than one interpretation can be true, then invite the class to turn to Tarrou's lengthy exposé of his beliefs and life story toward the end of the book (229–52; all page references are to the Gallimard 1947 edition). We read (the students read) this passage almost in its entirety, analyze Tarrou's statements, and generally conclude that, for him, the plague stands for evil. We then read the few short passages in which other characters variously define the plague as "life" and as "death." We look at Rambert's interpretation of the plague as "the necessity to keep starting over." These analyses and comparisons of passages continue until we reach a consensus that "evil" is the most likely meaning. Since evil can take many forms and since, in the context of Camus's "*Absurd*," death itself might be regarded as a manifestation of evil, this interpretation seems to me the soundest because it is the most inclusive and therefore the most useful pedagogically as well as philosophically. Philosophically because the imperative to recognize the existence and the presence of evil is at the very center of existentialist thought; pedagogically because it permits us to examine from the same angle all the characters and all the points of view they represent.

The major characters—Rieux, Tarrou, and Rambert—reduce evil to a comprehensible scale so that average people are in a position to oppose it. They see its manifestations in suffering and injustice, two facts of human life familiar to all and characteristic of every intolerable circumstance, from an innocent child being devastated by disease to a prisoner being tortured or executed. Evil then becomes common and ordinary (Hannah Arendt's phrase "the banality of evil" comes to mind), and we can no longer make excuses not to fight it. And not only evil, but the struggle itself is shown as almost dull. Dull but imperative. Why Rieux, Tarrou, Grand, and, eventually, Rambert accept this task without glory or glamour and how they go about accomplishing it is the focal point of our discussions. The long passage, already mentioned, in which Tarrou expresses his sentiments is our starting point. Once we have clarified the meaning of the "plague," we return to this passage, then read and analyze the positions taken by the other major characters in the series of conversations between Tarrou and Rieux (126–31, 244–55), Tarrou, Rieux, and Rambert (162–65, 207–09), and Rieux and Rambert (87–91, 151–53). In all these exchanges, I pay particular attention to the quiet tone and to the modest, almost self-effacing attitude of the characters, for I think that it is mainly through this stylistic device that the banality of evil is established and made convincing. Again, this reduction is essential if all—a Grand as much as a Rieux—are to consider themselves capable and obligated to join in the struggle. All are shown as equals, equal in their humanity, sharing an equality conferred by death. The reduction is also necessary if one is to escape the errors of such respectable doctrines as humanism and Christianity. If the humanists are helpless before the plague, it is because they do not believe it exists. They do not believe it exists because they cannot conceive of it on a "human" scale (42–43). If Paneloux's

prayers are inefficacious to fight the plague or to offer protection, it is because
Christianity justifies its existence by finding explanations for the plague (95–
102). If divine intervention is the cause, it can be the only cure. //

What, then, separates those who refuse to recognize the plague and struggle against it from those who accept the burden? We look at the ways in
which the protagonists experience the phenomenon of the "*prise de conscience*": Rieux's disquiet early in the story, Tarrou's revulsion by the death
sentence and its execution, and Rambert's slowly awakening comprehension.
Analyzing how each of these characters becomes aware (*prend conscience*)
allows me to connect the themes and ideas of *La Peste* to other works by
Camus as well as to related concepts in the work of the other authors studied.
Rambert's explanation of his initial reactions to the catastrophe, "I felt a
stranger to this city," is an invitation to compare the actors of this drama to
Meursault of *L'Etranger*, and the psychological resistance involved in feeling
"different," in being "*un cas d'exception*," to the theme of guilt and innocence
in *La Chute*. The passages dealing with the repetitiousness of the struggle
lead directly to *Le Mythe de Sisyphe*, and the ones insisting on the need to
accept this futility, without despair, to *L'Homme révolté*. Rieux's experience
of a "*léger écœurement*" reminds one of Roquentin's "*nausée*" in the novel
of that name by Sartre. The phenomenon of the *prise de conscience* itself
takes us back to one of our quotations from *Situations II* on the difference
between being born human and *becoming* fully so, while we are taken back
to the other quotation by Rieux's concluding remarks on his reasons for
writing this account of the epidemic. The artist must travel an additional
distance. A writer in particular must not only participate in the struggle but
must also bear witness.

By the time we reach the end of the course, students not only understand,
they have come to *feel* the distance that separates the objective and impersonal attitude espoused by Romain Rolland and Jules Romains from existential commitment. They discern the intellectual kinship among the authors
we have studied, which confers a sense of unity not only on this philosophically oriented literary movement but on the course itself. The final discussions of *La Peste* focus once more on defining the "plague." Taking into
account the slightly divergent views of all the major characters, we conclude
that conquering the plague does not mean only obliterating the immediately
threatening germs, always a temporary victory at best, but just as urgently,
it means becoming forever ready to start over, by conquering the urge to
resign ourselves to fate, by resisting the temptation to acquiesce. The students' original response proves correct. Of all the works they have read, *La
Peste* offers the most credible models for decent conduct, even while the
quest for an absolute might continue. They find in *La Peste* the assurance

that the futility of human endeavor does not diminish us but elevates us, and I believe that it is this reassuring affirmation, expressed in an understated yet eloquent style, that is responsible for the work's universal appeal.

BIBLIOGRAPHICAL REMARKS

Whenever available, all the books used in this course are from Gallimard's Folio series, because of its large print, attractive appearance, and reasonable cost.

When, in addition to my explanatory remarks, quotations are also used to teach the concept of *unanimisme*, they are taken from Jules Romains, *Mort de quelqu'un*, or, when a lighter touch seems desirable, from Romains, *Knock*. Quotations to illustrate Rolland's notion of living *au-dessus de la mêlée* come from Romain Rolland, "Au-dessus de la mêlée."

As I mentioned in the text, students are discouraged from reading secondary sources. But I have found that, besides the standard critical material available on individual authors, two books that can be very useful to the instructor for cogent arguments on both sides of the issue of *engagement* are Julien Benda, *La Trahison des clercs*, and Everett W. Knight, *Literature Considered as Philosophy*.

The Centripetal Structure of Camus's *La Peste*

Jennifer Waelti-Walters

Much has been written about the power of *La Peste*, and the major concern is almost always with the book's moral force. To such an end the critic or commentator examines the thoughts and actions of all the major characters one by one, the predominant images, and the symbolic possibilities of the work; yet a study that pulls all these elements together is difficult to find. And this omission is curious, for the book derives its moral power largely from the centripetal strength of its structure as a novel.

La Peste is structured dramatically in five acts (see fig. 1), with the turn-around, as usual, coming at the end of the third section. The first three sections show the increasing sweep of death and a resulting loss of individuality, from the failed suicide of Cottard to the mass burials in part 3. In contrast, part 4 deals with resurrection in many forms. The myth of Orpheus, he who goes to the realm of the dead and emerges unscathed, is used to underline the scandal of death when the actor playing Orpheus collapses on stage. Then, although the innocent child dies, his fight is a long one; and shortly thereafter Rieux and Tarrou are revitalized by their swim. We must believe that Paneloux dies so that he may be reborn. Grand recovers. Rats reappear. Then part 5 brings the necessary denouement.

As in *Le Malentendu*, Camus is using the form of a classical tragedy so that all the cultural baggage of the structure—a sense of human grandeur and the weight of the daily struggle against fate—may be brought to bear on the absurdity of the situation in which his characters find themselves. In the play the friction between Camus's plot and characters and the expectation created by the form builds malaise and frustration in the audience. In *La Peste* the pace of the tragedy is not that of a play, but the sense of doom thus generated adds depth to Rieux's chronicle. This structure shapes the presentation of the major theme, death, and cuts directly through the book. The other themes—love, condemnation, and communication—are sub-concerns born of the major theme and circle around it in a different formation.

La Peste has a basic cyclical structure (fig. 2). The plague starts in April of one year, grows with the increasing heat, and weakens as the weather becomes colder, finally disappearing from sight in February of the following year. The circle is not closed, however, because, as we are told in the last words of the novel, the action of the plague can flare up again at any time to start a new cycle of destruction—a cycle whose movement is reinforced by the description of the plague as a flail turning around in the air above

Figure 1.

Part I	**Part II**	**Part III**
Rieux's wife		
Private separations	Public separation	Burial
Illness becomes plague	Remedies:	(1) in ground
First death	(1) administrative	(2) in memory
Cottard	(2) physical	Cottard
	(3) practical	
	(4) religious	
	First sermon	
	Town closed	

Part IV	**Part V**
	Town open
Wrongness of death	End
(1) *Orpheus*	(1) of separation (final)
(2) child	(2) separation
Resurrection	Tarrou's death
(1) swim	Rieux's wife
(2) Grand	Cottard
Second sermon	
Paneloux's death	

Figure 2.

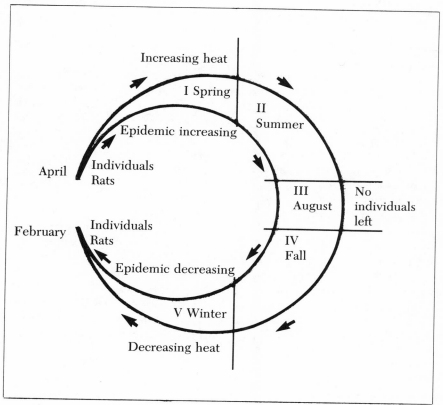

Oran and by the whistling noise of which Rieux is frequently conscious as
his sensitivity to the situation increases.

   The circular movement in time is supported by a clearly defined suggestion
of geographical centrality if not of total circularity. The city is walled and
gated; it sits in the middle of a plateau, surrounded by mountains and sea.
Railway lines and marine routes bring traffic in from all sides, and the trams
bearing the dead run around the outside edge of the city, along the cliffs.
Meanwhile, within it, Rambert, who wants to escape physically, gravitates
out from the center to the walls of the city, whereas Tarrou and Rieux, as
their friendship develops, move up and in to the high point from where
they can see the sea. The crowds mill around in the enclosed space.

   Meanwhile the chronicle itself, in an all-encompassing development, starts
with a description of individuals (Rieux's wife, Cottard, Michel) and the

remedies offered to them, gradually shifts to the group of doctors and their official remedies that are applied to all, moves on to impersonal collectivities (the hospitals, quarantine camps, and mass graves), and finally returns to the individuals who are still alive at the end of the story. Thus a circular movement is created within the narrative itself.

Within this organization of time, space, and narrative, the very characters themselves are disposed in a series of circular structures. We may say that death by plague is the center and that all the characters are concerned with it in one way or another, as illustrated by the grouping of all the major characters around the hospital bed of the dying child. All, that is, except Cottard, with whom we shall deal later, for his absence is indeed part of the structure, as is the absence of active women in the story.

Most of the characters turn around Bernard Rieux. Each of the major ones shares one of his concerns and usually develops it further than he does (fig. 3). Thus Tarrou is linked to Rieux by their sense of the absurd; Paneloux by their fight against evil; Rambert by their desire to find happiness with the women they love; Grand by their inability to express their feelings; Castel by their desire to cure the sick; and Othon by their sense of law and order. In this way the words and actions of each character become part of Rieux's own struggle to act against the plague and to understand it.

Similarly, the possibilities of the silent relationships Rieux has with his wife and mother are drawn out and explored a little by the relationships given to the other characters (fig. 4). Rieux is separated from his wife. From

Figure 3.

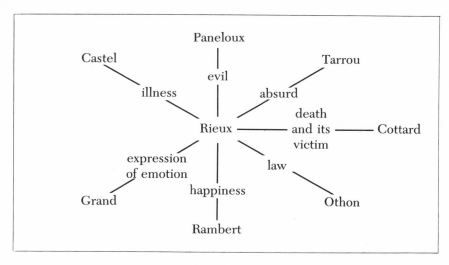

Figure 4.

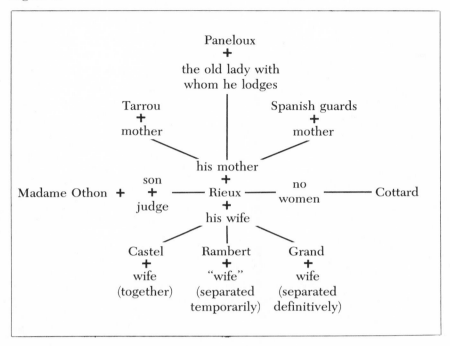

the scene at the station we learn that all is not well between them. Indeed her illness—tuberculosis—would tend to give a symbolic representation of their relationship for it is traditionally considered in literature to be an illness that strikes a passionate individual and is thus totally opposed to the collective and punitive aspect of plague (see Sontag 20–22, 26–36, 37, 39–41, 58, 71). We are left with the suggestion that they love each other but that they have not been communicating well. They believe (ironically) that all will be well in the future.

Rambert's separation from the woman he loves, his urgent desire to go to her, and his eventual renunciation of individual happiness in order to struggle for the general good are contrasted directly to Rieux's behaviour. We are left to wonder whether Rieux, too, wishes to join his wife and whether he loves her as Rambert loves his mistress. Interestingly, it is Tarrou, not Rieux, who tells Rambert about Rieux's wife. The doctor himself chooses to talk to Grand. Thus an obvious link is created between Rieux's situation and that of the old man who lost his wife because he omitted to tell her he loved her. Rambert's temporary separation and Grand's permanent one draw attention to Rieux's situation, which is in between; though Rieux thought he and his wife would not be apart for long, he may well lose her before he can express his love to her. Two further developments complete the treatment of the situation: Mme Castel comes back into the city to join her husband, though no one had ever thought that they were a particularly devoted couple, and Judge Othon finds himself lost without his wife, though he was barely civil to her when they were together.

Rieux's relationship with his mother is deep and unspoken; it, too, finds echoes in the lives of the other characters. Tarrou had a silent mother whom he loved deeply and who lived with him until her death. Her memory is the basis for his attachment to Mme Rieux. Rambert finds a surrogate mother in the old Spanish woman in whose house he stays. She looks after him materially, and her comment that he wants to escape for sexual reasons because he does not have anything deeper to believe in touches the crux of his position and helps him decide to stay in Oran. Paneloux also has a surrogate mother in the old woman in whose house he lodges, but his relationship with her is the opposite of Rambert's. He offends the old lady and refuses to explain his attitude and behaviour. She watches over him in silence and finally calls the ambulance in order to do her duty.

Thus the active, thinking men are surrounded by a circle of silent, still, and caring women who are, in effect, absent. There are no active women in the book at all. The young women are not there, and the old, though apparently loving, do not communicate with their menfolk. Whether considered in the context of the absurd or war or evil, this is a curious state of affairs that only becomes apparent when we look at the structure of the novel and that focuses our full attention on the men in the story while binding them more closely together.

An uncharitable explanation of the situation might be that Camus, faithful to North African customs, French philosophical tradition, and the practice of the Roman Catholic church, did not think of women as either active or thinking beings. (We notice that Paneloux inevitably addresses his congregation as "mes frères," though only the second time are we told that it is a men's mass.) This attitude is certainly explained partially by reference to his own life: his mother was deaf and silent, and he was separated from his wife during the war; hence women were essentially absent from his life and love remained unexpressed.

This almost total silence is particularly interesting, however, when we consider that the men show themselves quite capable of communication (fig. 5). Certainly, it is always a struggle for Grand to find the right words to express himself, but he does finally write his letter to Jeanne. All the others write regularly during the plague: Tarrou keeps a notebook; Paneloux prepares two sermons and does research, as does Castel. Rambert is a jour-

Figure 5.

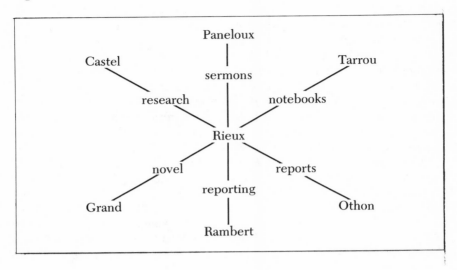

nalist and so, of course, he has no trouble in this respect; he is just temporarily prevented from writing by the situation. And Rieux is supposed to have written the chronicle we have read, so we must assume that his silence concerns his personal emotions only.

Again we see that the men are grouped around Rieux, offering us a variety of texts, all of which have something in common with Rieux's testimony: Castel offers medical research; Rambert describes facts in a form intended to interest the public; Tarrou makes observations and personal comments for his private use; Grand goes one step further and expresses his concept of the world as fiction; Paneloux draws theological and moral precepts from what he experiences. Each in his own way offers a description of the plague. Rieux's work incorporates all his friends' forms of writing except fiction, and fiction is, of course, present in the very form of *La Peste*. Hence the male characters circle around Rieux yet again, providing comment on his activity.

Through this recurrence in the structure, the three levels of Rieux's life and action—his struggle against the plague, his feelings, and his writing— are enriched, varied, and called into question by the concerns and actions of the other characters, giving the novel great density of texture.

The one character who has not been accounted for in all this is Cottard. Curiously enough, he would seem to offer a negative image to Rieux's positive one. Cottard seeks death at the beginning and never fights it; in this way he is for the plague and against Rieux's conception of medicine. He is against the law whereas Rieux is for it, as illustrated in what they do for Rambert. Cottard writes nothing, has no job, no convictions, and no women in his life. He aims only to survive in the crowd whereas Rieux stands alone.

Being the opposite of Rieux is not Cottard's only role in the novel, however. He takes his place with Judge Othon, the asthmatic old Spaniard, and the man who spits on cats in a subsidiary group of characters described by Tarrou in his notebook. Judge Othon interests Tarrou because he, like Tarrou's father, condemns people to death in the name of society; Cottard is the judge's victim. Cottard is a living version of the red-haired man Tarrou saw the first time he went to court. He is a condemned man, and, just as Tarrou followed the first case in the newspaper, so he interests himself in Cottard's activities and reactions. Tarrou's interpretation of his situation in life—that it is impossible to act without taking the risk of being responsible for someone's death—is the root of his interest in all the people around him. The catman is the first person he sees who is probably not hurting anybody by his actions, but he proves vulnerable to changing circumstances and disappears. In the old Spaniard who stays in bed all day, Tarrou finds a better example of what he is seeking. In his view the old man's repeated actions protect him from all risk of being a judge and possibly make him a saint (fig. 6).

By this subsidiary group Tarrou and Rieux are pulled even closer together. Not only does Tarrou have a place in the group around Rieux, but Cottard and Othon have a role to play in each of the groups. The whole structure is thus rendered more complex, and Tarrou is given preeminence among the men around Rieux.

It is Rambert who says at the end of part 2: "Je vous dis que ça consiste à recommencer." This pattern of recurrence is everywhere in the novel, from Rieux's and Tarrou's daily struggles against the epidemic to Rambert's attempts to leave Oran, Paneloux's two sermons where the second reworks the ideas of the first, Castel's search for an effective serum, and Grand's rewritten sentence to the trains going back and forth to the crematorium

Figure 6.

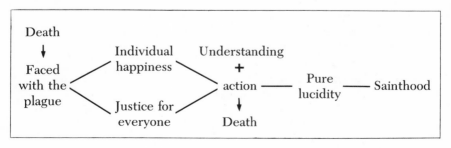

and the old Spaniard transferring his peas from one saucepan to another. Every significant action in the novel is done over and over again with the same regularity as the movement of the flail turning above the city.

As we have seen, the group of vocal men and the group of silent women turn around Rieux throughout the novel. The men share his concerns and his activities, and in one way or another they are made in his image. (Indeed all except Grand are described in a similar physical way—solidly built and fairly young.) In this way all their actions direct our attention through themselves to Rieux. The women serve the same function, for they bind the men by a passive bond of silence, separation, and waiting; the mother figures live through their menfolk and suffer for them, the wives are absent. Again figures and context are linked directly to Rieux.

The doctor is therefore the unquestioned center of the novel, and at the end, when he claims to be the voice both of the individual and of the collectivity, he becomes the circumference also. In Rieux himself we find both the structure of the novel and the symbol of that structure; he is the focus of forces emanating from the other characters as well as the active force within the chronicle and the generating force of the narrative itself. The power of La Peste comes not only from Rieux's moral standpoint but also from his role within the literary tissue of the work, for never is any element of the book allowed to preempt his presence. The women are all reduced to shadows, and the men are all variations on the main character. The unwaveringly centripetal structure of La Peste is one of the major keys to its strength.

I try to make this structure clear in the classroom by using the diagrams shown here in the three final hours of a ten-hour sequence on La Peste. The students have already read the whole book, and I have taken them through the text six times. Each time I have pointed out and commented on every reference to one character only, starting with Rieux and moving on to Tarrou, Paneloux, Rambert, Grand, and Cottard. (I teach La Peste in a second-year French literature course, which is both the first real literature course the students take and the first taught entirely in French. Upper-year students might be expected to move more swiftly through this first stage.) Thus it is not until the students understand the development of each character as a separate entity with his own internal logic that I begin to talk about the structure of the novel and what the structural information adds to our comprehension both of this work and of Camus's thought. I draw the diagrams on the board, developing the argument outlined in this chapter as I go, adding diagram to diagram until the whole complex pattern becomes evident.

My aim is to show students that an author provides them with a variety of information and that the story line and the dialogue are only the surface manifestations of a much more subtle piece of communication. I find that I cannot do this if I hand out the diagrams. It seems essential that the class see the structure grow out from the characters they have studied, so that they can understand each structure before the next is superimposed on it. When presented in these cross-sections, the technical density of the novel is less daunting, and students acquire a sense of novelistic structure—a sense that books, like people, have skeletons under their smooth surfaces. Finally, all being well, they realize the strength that the underlying patterns give to the work and understand the impact that the centripetal movement toward the protagonist and the implacable march of death across the repetitions have on the "message" of *La Peste*.

A Method of Presenting Albert Camus's *The Plague*

Irma M. Kashuba, S.S.J.

The following presentation is intended for undergraduate students of French, primarily upperclassmen who have some knowledge of French literature, world literature and history. It is an introductory lecture; students would subsequently be expected to contribute to class discussions on the three levels of meaning, on the characters, and on the language. They would analyze passages indicated in the course of the presentation and give reports on some major critics, such as Quilliot, Brée, Onimus, Cruickshank, and Thody. Finally, they would write a report on a major aspect of the novel. Possible topics include Camus's satire of forms of oppression; the theme of separation; style and images; character portrayal, for example, Tarrou and Rieux as two faces of Camus; moral implications of *La Peste*; Camus's image of the absurd; time and space in the novel; comparison with other works read, for example, the theme of *ennui* in Bernanos and Camus; Camus's concept of the hero. Normally this presentation would come at the end of a course in twentieth-century French literature or in a seminar where such themes as satire or the hero unite the course.

For the student of the 1980s, the classical world may seem very remote. Yet those who have read Thucydides' *History of the Peloponnesian Wars* will find a familiar ring in Albert Camus's modern novel *La Peste*. In book 2, chapters 48–53, Thucydides tells of a plague that befell ancient Athens, of unknown origin or remedy. Usually fatal, it was marked by despondency and rapidity. People crowded into cities, only hastening the dire effects of the malady. They grew reckless of all law and gave themselves up to the pleasures of the moment. Bodies were heaped everywhere, even in temples, and common burial pits were rapidly hollowed out. Everywhere the plague gave rise to dejection and despair.

It is not surprising that Albert Camus should follow the classical tradition so closely. In fact, the reader can almost parallel Thucydides' sentences with Camus's description of the plague. Camus has also used other ancient sources that contain descriptions of a plague: Sophocles' *Oedipus the King* and Aeschylus' *The Suppliants*. The book of Exodus in the Bible tells of many plagues. Everywhere the description is the same. Medical books, which Camus carefully consulted, list symptoms not unlike Thucydides'. Camus traces the plague throughout history, especially in the Middle Ages, quotes Defoe in his epigraph, and has read Herman Melville. *La Peste* in 1947 is modern as Sophocles twenty-four centuries before is modern, for Camus has resurrected a universal myth that addresses a universal problem, with classical economy and distance.

La Peste can be read on several levels. The three most important are the literal, which matches classical and scientific descriptions of the plague; the political, which has obvious echoes of the Occupation from 1941–44; and the metaphysical, which addresses the problem of evil in the world. The modern student, like the modern critic, will discover others: the psychoanalytic, as Alain Costes has carefully delineated in *Albert Camus et la parole manquante: Etude psychanalytique*; the narcissistic, explored by Brian Fitch in *The Narcissistic Text*; and the linguistic, examined by Paul Fortier and Gerald Prince.

The literal level is not without importance, for it provides the "chronique" that Camus calls his work. Rats emerge from everywhere and nowhere, slimy and slippery, like the purging of a putrefying substance. With characteristic impassivity the narrator reports their numbers: 6,231 on 25 April, for example (16; all page references are to Livre de Poche edition). We read of the first symptoms of the plague: the infected person vomits a rosy bile, has swollen neck glands, and suffers an intense burning sensation. The victim dies within forty-eight hours (43). When the plague is formally declared, the city is cut off from communication with the outside world. During the third week 302 people die (out of 200,000 inhabitants), a figure that means nothing to the frightened populace. In June the number mounts with the raging Mediterranean sun to 120 each day. No one may enter or leave the city; tourism is ruined; companies begin to suffer financial losses, a problem ironically suggested as one of the worst signs of the plague.

Tarrou, Rieux, Grand, and later Rambert and Père Paneloux form "équipes sanitaires" to combat the plague. People living in groups are dispersed. Curfew is rigorously enforced. Burials are like the ones described by Thucydides: rapid and communal. Toward the end of the plague, no one, not even family, can attend the burial ceremonies; mourners simply sign the register the following day. Burial is finally replaced by cremation. After several notable victims —Père Paneloux, Tarrou, and the young son of Judge Othon—the plague subsides, in the month of January. But, Camus concludes, the plague never dies or disappears. It only sleeps and can reappear at any time.

Indeed a plague did reappear, the plague of oppression, and it was to symbolize oppression in all its forms that Camus wrote the book, as he told Roland Barthes in his letter of 1955 (*Œuvres* 1: 1965–67). Critics contemporary with Camus hailed the novel as a parable of the German Occupation. Since Camus conceived the idea in 1938 and began to work on it in 1943, he evidently did have the Occupation in mind. Frenchmen during this period called the German presence "la peste brune." The "univers clos" of Oran, sealed off from all communication, is not unlike the France of the early 1940s, which like Oran monotonously pursued its daily occupations, yet remained subconsciously aware of a threatening presence. The "équipes sanitaires" organized by Rieux and his friends are like the small groups of the Resistance in which Camus himself participated. The rationing of food and gas, the careful use of electricity, all evoke wartime measures.

The difficulty with this parallel is in the application of moral values, as has been pointed out by critics such as Cruickshank (*Camus* 176), McCarthy (229), and Thody (*Camus: A Study* 34). The plague is presented as an absurd force of unknown origin, not the willful violence of war killings and the inhumanity of the Occupation. In fact, the moral problem continued, in the Arab population that Camus seemed deliberately to exclude from his novel. Conor Cruise O'Brien sees the rats returning eight years later "from the quarter in which the narrator had refused to look: from the houses which Dr. Rieux never visited. . . . The source of the plague is what we pretend is not there" (59). Neither the Occupation nor the Algerian revolt may touch today's student, yet currently other prisons and exiles threaten civilization: Soviet labor camps, Central American guerillas, colonialism in the third world, economic and technological warfare, totalitarian ideologies. If the student can make these parallels, Camus's novel has already proved itself a classic.

Besides incarnating a "vast concentration camp" (Quilliot 137), the novel also presents Camus's particular articulation of the absurd in 1947. He expresses the absurd in "la lutte contre la création telle qu'elle était" (102), in the refusal to accept the suffering of children, namely the death of Judge Othon's son, that he shares with Dostoevsky's Ivan Karamazov, and in the hatred of capital punishment that haunts Tarrou. Camus's absurd also includes being condemned for an unknown crime and being trapped in a situation that one did not choose, like Rambert who arrived in Oran by accident. Yet one must never resign oneself to "ce qu'on ne peut pas comprendre." (174). This refusal to accept being condemned to the absurd struck critics of the 1950s and 1960s, together with the implicit message of fraternity contained in the novel. At least six times in the book Camus insists that we are all involved, "la peste fut notre affaire à tous." Yet Camus once again does not solve the moral question, for he equates evil with a plague that comes from unknown sources; similarly, he sees ignorance as the source of human unhappiness. His is a moral of relativity yet of logical honesty. His Pascalian "angoisse" does not seem to admit "que le cœur a ses raisons que la raison ne connaît point."

Any work of fiction articulates its ideas through its structure, characters, and language. Thus Camus's three levels of meaning take on the form of characters like Rambert, Rieux, and Tarrou; they are circumscribed by his peculiar use of space and time, and they conform to his stylistic impersonality yet deep sensibility. *La Peste*, Camus's major work, which brought him instant popularity and wealth and helped win him the Nobel Prize in 1957, has been listed under many genres. Some see it indeed as a novel, perhaps a "nouveau roman" like Robbe-Grillet's *La Jalousie* (Fitch 23) or a Sartrian novel from which Balzac's omniscient narrator has been banned. Lazere calls it a naturalistic allegory (*Unique Creation* 173); Crochet, a myth; O'Brien, a sermon in the form of a fable, and Cruickshank, a symbol. Camus himself uses the word "chronique" several times in the course of the work.

The characters of the novel have fascinated critics. O'Brien limits them to three: the plague, the city, and the narrator (49). Others see them as stereotypes in a kind of morality play. None is Camus, but all are a part of him. All are dominated by one passion, which represents their attitude toward the plague. Accused by many, such as Lazere, of having created "noncharacters"—shadowy figures and symbols—Camus nonetheless has the talent to portray a person in a few lines, often in a few words.

Rambert, the journalist who came to Oran to study the Arab population and who is separated by the irony of fate from the woman for whom he lives, is "impatient du bonheur" (72). The most alive and convincing, he is one of Camus's most successful portraits. Joseph Grand, "qui ne trouve pas ses mots" (39), may incarnate the whole artistic sense of the work (Fitch 15), the author's efforts and frustrations in writing, and the lover's inability to possess the person beloved. He never gets beyond the first line of his novel, as he never progressed beyond a handclasp in declaring his love for Jeanne. This steadfast worker, "qui n'avait rien d'un héros" (108), represents the virtue of quiet patience that Camus admired and the modern nonhero, not unlike Rieux, who is barely distinguishable from the crowd.

Cottard, "un personnage qui grandit" (155) uses the plague for his personal profit. Amazingly, Camus does not condemn him, exemplifying the non-judgmental ethic enunciated by Tarrou. Like Grand, Cottard writes with colored chalk on his door, a blackboard image that Fitch sees as narcissistic. Opposed to Cottard is the severe Père Paneloux, in life and in death a "cas douteux" (187). Camus considered *La Peste* his most anti-Christian work, and thus he presents this otherwise self-sacrificing priest as what Onimus calls a "tragic Christian" (53), one who sees the God of vengeance rather than the God of mercy. Camus himself, uneducated in Christian doctrine, began his acquaintance by studying Augustine and always saw Christianity as antihumanistic.

Tarrou and Rieux, whose accounts of the plague form the basis of the narrative, are perhaps two sides of the same person. Tarrou is much more complex, an "angoissé" in the tradition of Pascal and Kierkegaard, and is caught between the desire not to be a victim of the plague and the necessity of being one. His aim is to be "un saint sans Dieu" (204), an apostle of the new religion of humanism. Rieux, the author of the journal, "veut être un

homme" (205), wants simply to do his task in a human way. He is interested
not in the salvation of humanity but rather in its health. Like Grand, he is
not distinguishable from the ordinary crowd; he strives for the humanism
of everyday life.

These characters step into a definite world, the city of Oran, in a fairly
definite year, 194–. Rieux's journal gives specific dates: the first rats appear
on 16 April; the plague reaches its peak in June; it subsides on 25 January.
It ebbs and flows with the season: with the beating sun of summer that
extinguishes color and joy (91); with the fog and rain of September that
resemble the plodding feet (*piétinement*) of Oran's citizens (150); with the
deluges of rain that wash the sky and the city in November (195). (Such
passages—there are seven in all—make excellent *explications de texte*; they
use symbols poetically and reveal the deeper aspects of the story. Fortier
has made many valuable points about these passages.)

Yet in this novel there is no time. "Within this framework," observes
Germaine Brée, "and pitted against the even movement of outer time,
another time pattern emerges, an inner measure of consciousness and un-
consciousness which reflects the emotional value and human content of the
events described" (*Camus*, 1972, 107). Camus, like Proust, is more concerned about our indifference to time; we make time; it does not make us.

Camus describes Oran well, in the first few pages, with characteristic
irony. Not unlike the Ambricourt of Bernanos, Oran is devoured by the
plague of the twentieth century, "l'ennui." The city where Camus had lived
and met his second wife, Francine, becomes a faceless world. Arabs are
nonexistent. The sky descends as the plague mounts in density and closes
in the city like a Baudelairean "couvercle." Cars turn in circles, streets are
empty as if it were a holiday, and all the citizens become exiles "qui se
heurtaient sans cesse aux murs qui séparaient leur refuge empesté de leur
patrie perdue" (60). (Again, the first few pages of the novel and the first ten
pages of the second part are excellent passages for discussion and explication.)

Particularly for the student reading Camus in French, the style in which
La Peste is written stands out in contrast to his other works and to other
twentieth-century novels. It is banal, distant, and ironic. Words like "rien,"
"vide," "banal," "monotone" abound. Maquet calls *La Peste* "wilfully drab"
(75), and Quilliot sees it as "the epic of banality" (140). Conversation consists
of empty phrases of politeness; marriage even before the plague was "une
longue habitude à deux" (6). "Le petit vieux" who spits on cats and the old
asthmatic who methodically transfers peas from one receptacle to another
show futility, and perhaps evasion from reality. Life and the plague, like
abstractions, are boring, and "par leur durée même, les grands malheurs
sont monotones" (145).

Modern critics have especially analyzed Camus's method of creating banality and distance. Gerald Prince, who has studied Camus's use of verbs of speaking, finds *dire* the most prevalent and the *passé simple* the most common tense. These devices and several other techniques contribute to "la volonté de nivellement à la stratégie de *la Peste*, qui consiste à exalter la moyenne, la collectivité, la condition humaine dans ce qu'elle a de moins spectaculaire et de moins héroique" (105). Fitch sees the images of always rewriting the same letter, of composing elliptical telegrams, of Grand's rewriting the same sentence as exercises in impersonality. The narrator himself is nameless until the end, and even then he is hardly identifiable, except for Tarrou's brief portrait of two paragraphs (Fitch 26). By using Tarrou's diary as one of the sources of Rieux's already distant account, Camus creates "a story within a story within a story" (27) and moves us still further into a no-man's-, or everyman's, land.

In a manner somewhat reminiscent of Flaubert, Camus excels in subtle irony. Germaine Brée sees the whole event of the plague as a devastating experience that brings little in return (*Camus,* 1972, 101). Quilliot notes that, in contrast to Victor Hugo, Camus "reduces to the ordinary the most scandalous of events" (140). As already noted the primary significance of the plague to most people is that it ruins the tourist business. Hundreds have already died in the early stages of the plague, but the authorities will do nothing until the malady is officially named. The press is no help; one wonders if Camus's work for the underground newspaper *Combat* was not often futile, as the human condition is absurd.

Yet beneath this monotonous universe there is another element that cannot fail to strike the reader accustomed to symbolism and poetry. It is the image of deep sensuality and sensibility. The climate is always violent—burning sun or torrential rain. Fortier sees Camus's principal images as "maladie, claustration, excès et chaleur" (126–77). The sea and the sun, as in all Camus's Mediterranean works, are omnipresent.

As critics look at the novel with over thirty-five years of distance, the three levels examined at the beginning—the literal, the political, and the metaphysical—seem to ensure the permanence of the work less than does a sincere note of human compassion. The basic myth of the novel, says Crochet (175), is the story of Orpheus and Eurydice, enacted on the stage in the middle of the novel (159), at the precise moment when the plague claims the actor playing Orpheus himself; he falls off the stage, figuratively descending into the underworld of death, perhaps never to find his Eurydice. Thus separation, exile, and the desire for the person one loves are, as Camus says, "la souffrance principale de ce long temps d'exil" (54) and the principal themes of this work. Camus masterfully portrays the experience of emptiness, "ce creux que nous portions en nous" (58), as the most difficult one of the human condition.

Critics such as Quilliot (154) and McCarthy (229) have noted that there are almost no young women in the novel, yet woman is everywhere present as the symbol of the need for love and human bonds. Camus's language is basically one of warmth and human feeling. Underneath the cold and distant exterior, sensuality throbs, surfacing in the seven passages analyzed by Fortier. (These are excellent texts for students to analyze in the context of love and separation, as well as of the plague and its effects on the citizens. The passages are included in the appendix of Fortier's *Une Lecture de Camus*.)

Sensuality and poetry are very present in the evocations of the sea— "la mer, qu'il faut toujours aller chercher" (7); "seule la mer . . . qui témoignait de ce qu'il y a d'inquiétant et de jamais reposé dans le monde" (35)—and especially in the forbidden plunge into the sea by Tarrou and Rieux, "le fugitif instant de paix et d'amitié" (205). The search for sensuality is symbolized by Rambert's longing for the woman he loves and by Rieux's quiet awareness of his dying wife. Camus seems to say that the human condition inevitably consists of separation and exile but that the desire for communion with another gives it value and dignity: "Il est une chose qu'on puisse désirer toujours, et obtenir quelquefois, c'est la tendresse humaine" (241).

For those familiar with undergraduate students, it is obvious that this presentation is very distilled. It offers only introductory guidelines to the characters. Camus has many other passages that describe them, even though in a shadowy way. Students can be directed to amplify the portraits. The brief discussions about time and space, about the creation of distance, and about irony are especially interesting to develop. A good check on comprehension is the student's ability to perceive symbolism and irony.

Students in twentieth-century French literature would be expected to make parallels with Proust concerning the question of time and with Bernanos on the theme of ennui, as suggested in this presentation. They would also know Sartre and would be interested in the relation between the two authors at the time Camus wrote *La Peste*. Normally in an undergraduate course students would deal only with one major work of Camus; therefore, references to his other works are minimal. But because of Camus's continuing popularity, it is not unusual that students have read other works and can compare *La Peste* with *L'Etranger* and *La Chute*.

An interesting procedure for the teacher is to evaluate the response of students to the various levels of meaning in the novel. Critics seem to have passed through three stages: the direct application to the German Occupation; the metaphorical implications of the work; and finally, in the late 1970s and early 1980s, linguistic analysis of distance, irony, and a need for human compassion. No doubt the last one will touch today's student the most, for the Occupation is long past and metaphysical speculation is less attractive. Yet Camus, like Thucydides and Sophocles, seems to have a message for every age.

The Plague and Its Contracts

Eugenia N. Zimmerman

I have taught *The Plague* in two contexts: in a first-year literature course for students intending to specialize in French and at the fourth-year "Honours" level in courses dealing with French existentialism and with modern critical approaches to Sartre and Camus. What follows is an amalgam of how I have taught *The Plague* in the past, how I might teach it in the future, and what I find particularly useful about the novel for students of narratology and reader-reception theory.

I intend to consider *The Plague* in terms of the important critical metaphor of the "contract" or "contractuality," so characteristic of contemporary literary theory. This use of this metaphor is, of course, an example of analogical reasoning, and care must be taken to ensure that sufficient intellectual distance is maintained. If used prudently and with caution, however, it provides a powerful interpretive strategy for processing a text. Then, too, the notion of the contract that, in legal terms, is a promise can also be studied both in relation to the traditional social-contract theory concerned with political and philosophical discourse and to that part of contemporary speech-act theory dealing with promises.

The Plague *and Its Genres*

The Plague belongs to two genres. Its overt genre is the chronicle; its covert genre is the allegory or, more precisely, that very type of historical allegory so brilliantly defined in Daniel Defoe's preface to the third volume of *Robinson Crusoe*, the text from which Camus drew his epigraph for *The Plague*: "tis as reasonable to represent one kind of Imprisonment by another as it is to represent any Thing that really exists, by that which exists not." It is as an allegory that *The Plague* has most engaged critical attention, and two discussions that might prove useful for a consideration of the subject in class are Henri Morier's *Dictionnaire de poétique et de rhétorique*, which offers a classical, lucid introduction, and Maureen Gilligan's *The Language of Allegory*, which presents a more iconoclastic view.

The Notion of Contractuality

Any text may be approached as though it were the result of an agreement, a "contract" deriving from generic and cultural conventions shared by the implied author and his or her implied readers. The implied author, through use of generic codes and conventions, intertextual allusions, ideological as-

54

sumptions, and received opinions—Roland Barthes's *doxa*—promises: if you, the reader, read this book, you will find such and such. The implied reader, having already read many books of an apparently similar type, on the basis of habit and experience, expects: if I, the reader, read this book, I will find such and such.

A contract can be violated. The implied author flouts generic and cultural conventions and systematically frustrates the general reader's expectations. This procedure, of course, characterizes much avant-garde activity. Gradually, however, by an operation similar to the dialectics of thesis-antithesis-synthesis, as a particular phenomenon of the avant-garde gets assimilated into the cultural mainstream, so do the violations become integrated into the conventions they transgressed, replacing or modifying them, to become themselves the possible object of future transgressions. Jonathan Culler's *Structuralist Poetics: Structuralism, Linguistics and the Study of Literature* is one of many discussions of this process.

A contract can be accepted or refused, either partially or completely. To accept a contract is (1) to infer its existence from clues in the text and, possibly, from other sources and (2) to approve or endorse one or several or all of its aspects. To refuse a contract is (1) to fail to infer its existence from clues in the text or, possibly, other sources or (2) to infer its existence but refuse to approve or endorse one or several or all of its aspects.

A contract can also be modified or negotiated in the following sense: reading strategies may be evolved that permit the acceptable aspects of the contract to be foregrounded and the unacceptable aspects of the contract to be effaced. Much has been made in reader reception theory of the "gaps" in the text the reader is expected to fill. A complementary activity that permits the restructuring of the text by the reader through the creation of "gaps"—those aspects the reader does not wish to see—remains to be systematically discussed.

The Plague *and Its Contracts*

The Plague may be conceived of as a series of contracts, more or less inferable, more or less problematic. They constitute the promises inherent in the text and are as follows:

The Contract of the Title

The general conventions governing the relation between a text and its title are respected by its implied author: unlike, for example, the transgressive *La Cantatrice chauve*, the title directs the reader's attention to the significant aspects of the text. The specific use of the term "plague" in the title reinforces the metaphoric resonances already associated with the term in the culture that produced the text and that the implied readers share. Even a cursory examination of dictionaries of western European languages (French, English, German, etc.) will reveal instances of the term "plague" used in a nonliteral, nonmedical sense, and that might be an interesting exercise to propose to a class. The cultural sign so generated turns out to be something like "physical malady = moral malady," so it might also be useful to bring to the attention of a North American classroom, where one might hope to find at least some amateurs of vintage films, Elia Kazan's 1950 *Panic in the Streets*, a depiction of an incipient plague epidemic in New Orleans, which is predicated on an equation very much like the one above. Thus, since the plague is a disease traditionally charged with mythological, historical, cultural, and rhetorical accretions, it is reasonable to infer that the implied reader can recognize these accretions when they are presented in a work, as they are in those passages of *The Plague* dealing with historical occurrences of the epidemic and their ramifications. If such recognition can be depended on, then metaphorical and allegorical possibilities can be fully exploited. An illuminating study of this type of exploitation, albeit only minimally concerned with the plague as such, is Susan Sontag's *Illness as Metaphor*.

The Contract of the Epigraph

The epigraph, like the title it follows, represents the conventions of its genre; it is visually foregrounded, having a page to itself, and it provides the reader with an organizing principle for making sense of the text. More specifically, it provides the basic semiotic contract underlying the text as a whole: the plague represents (*aliquid stat pro aliquo*). For readers who recognize the source of the epigraph, it is particularly compelling, since Daniel Defoe not only defined historical allegory in connection with *Robinson Crusoe* (as we have already seen), he also wrote *A Journal of the Plague Year*. Thus, from the statement that the imaginary might legitimately signify the real, one is doubly urged to infer an obligatory corollary: the plague signifies something other than itself.

The Three Parts of the Plague as Sign

A classic description of the three aspects of the plague as sign is John Cruickshank's *Albert Camus and the Literature of Revolt*. We may or may not decide to emulate the critic's "voice" or interpretation, but it is difficult to see how we could refute the claim that these aspects are, in effect, present in the text; indeed, I would say that they constitute the offering of the text, the specific set of contracts the reader is requested to accept:

Plague = Plague. This contract, the "literal" level usually referred to in discussions of allegory, is an identity; the plague is or equals itself, "an imaginary epidemic . . . which supposedly afflicted Oran sometime in the 1940's . . . a particular event . . . in a geographical location . . ." (Cruick-shank, *Camus* 166). It would seem unreasonable for a reader to refuse to accept this contract in the sense of refusing to acknowledge that this is indeed the spatiotemporal framework of the "world" constructed by the text. If plague = plague in this sense is not accepted as a given of the text, how can reading even begin? The closest I could come in the critical literature to a repudiation of plague = plague was Jean-Jacques Brochier's extremely antagonistic *Albert Camus: Philosophe pour classes terminales.* Yet even here, it is less a refusal to acknowledge what is being offered as the literal foundation of the text; it is, rather, a refusal to acknowledge that plague = plague is being offered according to appropriate discursive conventions, in this case, the aesthetic ones of vividness and precision.

In another sense, however, it might be said that plague = plague is refused, ultimately if not initially. Readers are strongly invited, particularly in the academy, to quickly transcend this—presumably less interesting— "superficial" level for the—presumably more interesting—"deeper" levels of the gradually inferred, more figurative contracts.

Plague = Human condition (negative aspects). Just as plague = plague is the most precise and circumscribed of the three contracts, so plague = human condition (negative aspects), "a general picture of man's position in the universe, faced by the problem of evil and the necessity of suffering" (Cruickshank, *Camus* 166), is the most encompassing. It is an equivalence: an injunction that in the context of the narrative, the signifier (*signifiant*) "plague" is to be used interchangeably with the signified (*signifié*) "human condition (negative aspects)"; consequently, one may be appropriately sub-stituted for the other. Proof of the existence of this equivalence is derived, of course, from the process of inference operating throughout the reading of the text, but it is at last explicitly stated by the asthmatic old man in his final conversation with Rieux: in the Stuart Gilbert translation, "But what does that mean—'plague'? Just Life, no more than that" (283; Hamilton 1948 ed.). Not only has this declaration the assertive force characteristic of any aphoristic statement, it also appears near the end of the story, a strong strategic position in any narrative. It may thus be presumed to carry con-siderable weight, and one would reasonably expect that its influence on the reader would normally be proportionate. Then, too, the signified, "human condition (negative aspects)," as a class, approaches the universal; it may contain what is for practical purposes an almost unlimited number of mem-bers. It is so atopical and so ahistorical that to accept it as an appropriate signified commits the reader to very little that is specific. It does not entail the imposing on oneself onerous semantic constraints; a vague apprehension of the "meaning"—"negativity"—will do.

To be sure, there are readers one could easily imagine as being loath to accept such a contract, those, for example, holding either strong theistic or strong Marxist convictions. The former, whether or not their religion resembles that ascribed to Father Paneloux, might find plague = human condition (negative aspect) and its implied corollary—that the human condition is all we have—offensive to their belief in the afterlife and in redemption through suffering. The latter, who cleave to a linear and meliorist view of human history, would find in the very atopicality and atemporality that might help a general reader accept the contract a barrier to their acquiescence. But for this general, less ideologically committed reader, the text's exhortation to let the plague equal the negative aspects of the human condition should normally receive, all else being equal, an affirmative response.

Plague = *Occupation.* Neither as restrictive as plague = plague nor as general as plague = human condition (negative aspects), plague = occupation, derivable from "a series of indirect references to the German Occupation of France" (Cruickshank, *Camus* 166), is also an equivalency: in a given context, plague may appropriately be substituted for Occupation. This contract, at least for the work's original public, was one of the most controversial aspects of the novel, and it mobilized much polemic and critical energy in the late 1940s and the 1950s. For those of us considering *The Plague* thirty-eight years after its first appearance and in a North American context, it may more usefully be seen, I believe, as a paradigm of a basic problem in reader-reception theory: how and why does a given reader accept or refuse a given contract? what variables are involved? It is this problem I should now like to address.

	Plague (signifier)	=	Occupation (signified)
Origin:	1 nonhistorical nonhuman nonintentional	≠	1' historical human intentional

Remarks: (1) *Nonhuman* implies *nonintentional*: it is not customary for scientific discourse to ascribe intention or volition, as understood in a human context, to disease-causing organisms.

(2) Camus's plague, unlike the one chronicled in *A Journal of the Plague Year*, is *nonhistorical*, an imaginary event created for didactic purposes.

Traits: 2   =   2'

                   sequestration   sequestration
                   abnormality   abnormality
                   extremity   extremity
                   constraints   constraints

Remarks: These properties are considered in their most abstract, generalized form, as classes to which specific occurrences can be ascribed:
curtailment of freedom of movement, life and death situations, etc.

Reaction: 3   ≠   3'
                   medical,   military
                   prophylactic
                   (human vs.   (human vs.
                      nonhuman)   human)

Thus, whereas $2 = 2'$ $1 \neq 1'$ and $3 \neq 3'$. Consequently, in plague = Occupation, there is an analogical relation between signifier and signified, in
which one or more but not all of the properties of the signifier "plague" are
equal to one or more but not all of the properties of the signified "Occupation," rather than a homological relation between signifier and signified,
in which all the properties of the signifier "plague" would be equal to all
the properties of the signified "Occupation." The class formed by the signifier
and the class formed by the signified intersect, but they do not completely
coincide.

A reader who accepts the contract plague = Occupation is thus in effect
accepting as legitimate and sufficient an analogical relation, a partial identity,
a resemblance based on approximation, on "more or less," whereas a reader
refusing the contract plague = Occupation is in effect calling for a homological relation, a one-to-one relation of identity among all the properties of
the signifier and all the properties of the signified. The first reader has, in
effect, for whatever reason, established a system of priorities, a hierarchical
scale of values whereby the fact that $2 = 2'$ takes precedence over and
outweighs the fact that $1 \neq 1'$ and $3 \neq 3'$. By contrast, the second reader, in
effect, for whatever reason, has established an antithetical system of priorities, a hierarchical scale of values whereby the fact that $1 \neq 1'$ and $3 \neq 3'$
takes precedence over and outweighs the fact that $2 = 2'$.

One or another of these positions would usually surface either in the
discourse of readers belonging to the original public—late 1940s—or in that
of readers relatively close to them in time—1950s. To be sure, more or less

distance would be maintained, a particular voice would be more or less dispassionate depending on whether its owner considered himself or herself a disputant involved in polemical confrontation or an "objective"—usually academic—exegete engaged in observing textual phenomena. A good sampling of the more polemical interventions conforming to the position of my second reader can be found in Pol Gaillard's La Peste: *Albert Camus*. For the same position expressed according to the conventions of thematic criticism and academic commentary, Cruickshank's is perhaps the most lucid text.

Once again, what is being called into question is not the existence but only the legitimacy of a contract establishing the equivalency plague = Occupation. Both the first and the second reader have accepted the contract in the first sense of this verb as defined above; they have inferred and acknowledged its existence. The first reader has also accepted the contract in the second sense of "accept" as defined above; this reader approves of its formulation and considers it receivable. The second reader, on the other hand, has refused the contract in the second sense of "refuse" as defined above; this reader does not approve of its formulation or consider it receivable.

What variables might lead a given reader of *The Plague* to accept or refuse this contract? The implications of this question are central to reader-reception theory, yet I can, in this discussion, treat them only in part and in an overschematic way.

Authorial Intention, Ideology, and Reader Response

The question of intention in literature has been with us for decades and is still being passionately debated, as passionately as plague = Occupation was when the novel first appeared, and I do not intend to consider all the characteristics of this debate. Two aspects of the problem are particularly germane, however: (1) the reader's inference of the intentions governing a given text and (2) the reader's attitude to the axiological system, the "ideology" inferred from a given text. A reader may derive knowledge of authorial intention from the text alone, from other texts by the same author, from texts by other authors. According to the specific proclivities of a given reader, one or another of these sources would be considered more or less relevant, more or less authoritative.

I would use as an operating principle the following: if no particular impediments exist and all else is equal and no specific evidence to the contrary is offered or inferred, then a reader will tend to be guided by authorial intentions as the reader has understood or inferred them from the text or other sources. For example, my first reader might be particularly cheered by Camus's defense of plague = Occupation in his letter to Roland Barthes (*Œuvres* 1: 1973–75), whereas my second reader would probably see no reason to accord any more authority to this ancillary document than to the primary text itself.

A most significant impediment, of course, to acceptance of authorial intent would be the perception of a hostile ideology or an axiological system inimical to one's own. This question was addressed in Wayne C. Booth's *The Rhetoric of Fiction* and, more recently, systematically explored by Susan Suleiman in articles in *Poétique* and *Poetics Today*.

Generally speaking, readers have four options in taking a position vis-à-vis a given ideology inferred from a given text (or texts). These are (1) *for*, position (+): reader approves of or is attracted to the inferred ideology; (2) *against*, position (−): reader disapproves of or is repelled by the inferred ideology; (3) *neutral*, position (o): reader is indifferent to the inferred ideology, neither approving nor being attracted by it nor disapproving of nor being repelled by it; and (4) *ambivalent*, position (+ / −): reader is both attracted to and repelled by the inferred ideology. *Ambivalent* is a complex and problematic category, potentially the most interesting of the four, but spatiotemporal constraints compel me to leave it for a future date; *for*, *against*, and *neutral* are more amenable to schematic treatment. I do not conceive of these last three as discrete; rather they are to be plotted on a continuum, more or less (+), more or less (o), more or less (−). Thus, with the acceptance of a given contract in the second sense of these terms, it is when the reader is at or near the positions (+) or (o) that the operating principle enunciated above would function with little or no interference; however, if the reader is near or at the position (−), then the principle's functioning would be seriously perturbed. Once again, it is as though an implicit system of priorities were operating whereby a reader's ideological conviction took precedence over knowledge or inference of authorial intent in governing the acceptance or refusal of contracts organizing a text. Thus, with regard to *The Plague*, if I do not hold a position that requires the Occupation to be presented only in certain ways and if it is reasonably clear to me that plague = Occupation represents authorial intent, then even if I see that plague = Occupation is analogical rather than homological, unless I am also a logician or have little tolerance for metaphor in general, then there is no reason for me not to accept the contract. If ideological constraints are not operating, then aesthetic considerations might well play a more dominant role: I might consider that my reading would be enriched if I accepted the allegorical possibilities inherent in plague = Occupation and, correspondingly, that it could be seriously impoverished if I failed to do so.

If, on the other hand, I do have particular and strongly held convictions concerning the Occupation and how it should be represented and if these convictions are in some way called into question by plague = Occupation (or if I am particularly nice with regard to logical exactitude), then not only will my knowledge or inference of author's intent that plague = Occupation not be allowed to take precedence over my position ($-$), but I would consider such intent all the more heinous, an illegitimate source of an illegitimate contract.

The Reader's Position in Time and Space

If a novel represents a purely imaginary event for which little or no allegorical dimensions can be inferred from the text or acquired from other sources, it clearly differs from a novel such as *The Plague* in which an imaginary event, the plague, represents a historical event, the Occupation. For the non-allegorical novel, the question of ideology does not cease to exist, but it does not exist in the same way nor is it subject to the same set of constraints as it is in the allegorical novel. Once a historical event is in question, then a basic variable to be considered is the closeness or distance of a given reader to that event. In general, unless specific reasons to the contrary exist, the closer the position of the reader in time and space to a given historical event, particularly one so traumatic as the Occupation, the less likely that the reader's position on the ideological continuum would be near or at (o); the further the position of the reader in time and space from a given historical event, the more likely—or at least possible—that the reader's position would be near or at (o).

Thus, it is reasonable to expect that our particular implied readers, mostly North American adolescents, would be closer to (o) than Europeans of the 1940s and 1950s. Whether they accept plague = Occupation would most probably depend on (1) their skill in inferring intentions and contracts from the text and from other sources; (2) their response toward the analogical reasoning inherent in plague = Occupation, a student of analytical philosophy reacting differently perhaps from a student of creative writing; and (3) their suggestibility to authority and the authoritative discourse of the author, the commentators, and their instructors.

Perhaps our basic classroom strategy should be a moderate reader-reception theory in which we try to give everyone and everything their due, both the constraints of the text and the active collaboration of the reader. The text's constraints are not monolithic, but they are real. The reader's right to interpretation is considerable, but it is not unlimited. Particularly in the academy, some readings are more receivable than others. But the degree of receivability among readers today might well depend not on dicta emanating from on high but on patient and meticulous negotiation.

THE PLAGUE IN THE STUDY OF PHILOSOPHY, LAW, AND MEDICINE

Teaching *The Plague* in an Introductory Philosophy Course

Richard T. Lambert

This study concerns the use of two short selections from Albert Camus's novel *The Plague* in an introductory philosophy course taught during spring semester 1982 at Carroll College. Carroll is a four-year undergraduate liberal arts institution in Helena, Montana, affiliated with the Roman Catholic church and attended by some thirteen hundred students. Typical attendance at the course under review, PL 101, Perspectives in Philosophy, is thirty students a semester. Almost all of them are taking their first college philosophy course and probably experiencing their first sustained contact with philosophical ideas and methods.

Objectives of an Introductory Philosophy Course

The goal of any introductory course in philosophy is to provide students with their initial concentration on philosophical writing and thinking. Such a course generally employs one of two different approaches, historical (chronological order) or topical (order of subject matters). The topical approach may

63

be either "problematic," which aims at discussing issues, or "doctrinal," which proposes systematic solutions to issues. My approach in the course under discussion was problematic-topical, as it had been for many semesters of Perspectives in Philosophy.

The goal of my course was to acquaint students not only with philosophy but also with some of the great literature that constitutes the "humanities." Many entering (or even graduating) college students have no experience with classic literature (to say nothing of classic philosophical literature). Not all literature, of course, is of philosophical import, but some offers a readable and attractive gateway to the discussion of ideas. This premise of the philosophical value of literary pieces informed the textbook that I chose for the perspectives course and that I discuss later.

Using Camus in a Philosophy Class

In many respects the writings of Albert Camus represent a promising corpus for inclusion in an introductory philosophy course. The concrete contexts in his fiction, his fine literary style, his passionate existential concerns, and his lack of a technical vocabulary suit him to the general goal of an "initial concentration on philosophical writing and thinking." His spirit of questioning, exemplified in the notion of absurdity, fits well in a problematic approach oriented toward discussion of issues. And he fulfills the further goal of reading the humanities, since his best works are recognized modern standards that, it may be argued, embody a "classic humanism" (Lazere, *Unique Creation* 140, 232). While lacking the thorough analysis and systematic argument of most twentieth-century philosophy, Camus's work displays contemporary philosophy's skeptical tone and concentrates on the "meaning of life" issues currently enjoying a revival even in Anglo-American circles (see, e.g., Sanders and Cheney; Klemke); thus his writings have some claim on being "philosophical" literature. His potential for stimulation had been obvious to me in previous uses of *The Stranger* (in introductory and ethics courses), *The Rebel* (in Contemporary Philosophy), and *The Myth of Sisyphus* (in an introductory course). All these uses had seemed to stimulate the more thoughtful students, and *The Stranger* had proved a provocative favorite of almost everyone.

The Textbook

My use of Camus's *The Plague* was decided by my choice of textbook for the course. The text was Burton F. Porter, *Philosophy: A Literary and Conceptual Approach*, an anthology whose first edition I had used in an introductory course several years before. The attractions of this text were its accessibility to beginning students (the hardest selection was probably Immanuel Kant's *Groundwork of the Metaphysics of Morals*) and its combination of literary with philosophical selections. Porter's theory is that art can enhance and transmit philosophical visions and that art and philosophy are similar enterprises in their structural coherence and creative inventiveness (v–vii). He thus links fairly conventional philosophical works with literary pieces that supposedly express or involve the same ideas as their philosophical counterparts. For instance, Franz Kafka's *Metamorphosis*, with its assumption that one could retain one's personal identity even if transformed into a beetle, is paired with René Descartes's *Meditations*, which affirms the independence of the mind from the body.

The book divides into five sections: the concept of self (in which Kafka and Descartes appear); the problem of evil; free will and determinism; ethical ideals; and the nature of reality. This fifth section deals in "metaphysics," which "offers a characterization as to the basic nature of reality and indicates the response that is then appropriate for the conduct of our lives" (417). One metaphysical view is naturalism, which claims that all reality is explainable in natural terms; the illustrative selections are Stephen Crane's "The Open Boat" and Bertrand Russell's "A Free Man's Worship." Spiritualism identifies soul or spirit as ultimate; readings are from Hermann Hesse's *Siddhartha* and William James's *Varieties of Religious Experience.*

The last two readings in metaphysics are Camus's *The Plague* and Jean-Paul Sartre's *The Humanism of Existentialism.* They represent "existentialism," which

is a contemporary philosophy, embracing a metaphysical, epistemological, and ethical viewpoint. The existentialist maintains that man is a self-creating being who exists on earth with the consciousness to choose his own future, personally and collectively. The "essence" of a human being is not predetermined at birth but rather is formed by the decisions and commitments that are made during his lifetime. By crediting human beings with awareness and freedom of choice the existentialist regards man as having a spiritual part, but by stressing his physical position in a world without any discernible direction, the existentialist treats man as part of the natural not the spiritual universe. (418)

In a brief introduction (471) to the selection from *The Plague*, Porter identifies Camus as "one of the leaders of the existentialist movement" who sounded "some of the principal themes of existentialism, including absurdity, meaninglessness, anguish, freedom, despair, and commitment." By contrast with the "individualistic" existentialism of *The Myth of Sisyphus*, the "humanistic" existentialism of *The Plague* teaches that "Although we all live meaningless lives in a metaphysical sense, devoid of any ultimate cosmic purpose, we can try to help rather than harm one another. In this way, Camus believes, we will fully exist as human beings."

Porter's selection from *The Plague* juxtaposes two distantly separated passages. The first, from chapter 7 of part 2, is a conversation between Dr. Bernard Rieux and Jean Tarrou as the plague's grip on Oran is reaching its height; Father Paneloux has just preached his sermon charging the plague to the guilt of the populace. As the passage opens, Tarrou asks Rieux whether he believes in God. Rieux declares his indifference to theological matters and his conviction of the value of saving lives in an infuriatingly imperfect world. He accepts the transiency of any victories he might win against disease and cites his experience of "suffering" as the source of his wisdom.

The second passage, from part 4, chapter 6, presents a conversation between Rieux and Tarrou at a much later stage of the plague. Tarrou relates his personal history regarding the wider "plague" of selfish indifference; his awakening came in his sympathy for a prisoner condemned to death through the energies of Tarrou's prosecutor father. Yet, he admits, his rebellion against the established order approved of many deaths in the name of the political cause, and his side came to compete with the opposing side in rate of murder. Tarrou's personal solution is a humanitarian sympathy that eschews history-making projects in favor of a minimalistic but effective avoidance of death-dealing schemes. He wishes he could attain the next level and be a "true physician," a "saint without God"; but Rieux cautions that the most appealing prospect is that of simply "being a man."

Classroom Presentation of The Plague

The analysis of my pedagogy in teaching *The Plague* begins with some basic facts concerning the format and requirements of Perspectives in Philosophy, next states the rationale for the requirements, and then (in "Evaluation" section) assesses the effect of the pedagogy on students.

The daily format of this course was the following: assigned reading, instructor's presentation on the reading, class discussion. The selection from *The Plague*, which was only one out of some twenty reading assignments over the semester, could have no more than one class day devoted to it. The course required five activities of students: class attendance, daily reading assignments, daily quizzes on the reading, three full-period examinations, and a five-page report on the entirety of one work from which a selection appeared in the course. The announced objectives of the course were that students be able to: (1) appreciate both literary and philosophical texts and differentiate the two; (2) relate and compare different philosophical positions; and (3) evaluate philosophies logically and morally.

The five course activities were intended to coordinate with the three objectives. The appreciation mentioned in the first objective could, obviously, occur only if the students did the reading; each reading selection was therefore clearly announced in the previous class session, and an orally dictated short-answer quiz tested whether students had at least a cursory familiarity with the material. (A sample quiz question was: Why did Tarrou's father arise very early on certain mornings?) The book report was intended to foster a deeper and more sustained appreciation of the elected work's content and construction.

The examinations were special incentives to perform the relation and comparison demanded in the second objective. One examination question asked students to compare the atheisms of Camus, Sartre, and Russell; and another asked whether Camus in *The Plague* really did, as the textbook editor had claimed, take an "existentialist" position on the issue of "the nature of reality." Regular attendance at classes, while a patent condition for any type of success in the course, especially related to the second objective; for my presentation of any selection would include many references to other selections in the book and to related outside topics. Attendance also provided students with an example of the third objective, in my critical assessment of each author taken up.

Besides these announced course activities, more informal aspects of my pedagogy were also designed to motivate and test student reading. Perhaps most important was my overt enthusiasm for the selections, which I hoped would stimulate students to regard the readings as worthy literature. I provided them with some literary and historical context for each reading; for Camus, this consisted of brief background on his earlier thought (*Myth* and *Stranger*), on *The Rebel*, and on his relationship with Sartre. I attempted to encourage students' comparisons and reactions by contrasting the Rieux-Tarrou humanitarian atheism with traditional Christian beliefs on suffering, divine omnipotence and providence, and immortality. While this comparison could be used anywhere to make a point of general cultural interest, I thought it especially pertinent at a Catholic institution.

Evaluation

Let me now assess how well the selection from *The Plague* fulfilled the objectives of Perspectives in Philosophy. This evaluation considers the course objectives already mentioned as well as the term papers written on *The Plague*. The evaluation is based on my own recollection of the class day on

Camus and of later student work and on an informal survey of a representative sample of the students, conducted some six months after the course.

Reading and appreciation of classic texts in the humanities.   *The Plague* provided an adequate reading selection, although not the favorite one. The quiz indicated that the students did read the selection with at least superficial understanding. Those surveyed in the questionnaire agreed that the reading had been quite comprehensible. About half the students admitted interest in reading the novel further, and a good number chose *The Plague* for their book reports. But the book generated neither the intensity of interest nor the passion to finish that *The Stranger* had produced in earlier students, nor did it generate among them an intellectual discussion comparable to that which, in my teaching experience, had usually followed *The Rebel.*

Initiation into philosophical writing and thinking.   The selection from *The Plague* came across to students as philosophical literature and, because of its clarity and existential themes, as an appropriately introductory representative of philosophy. Students could see the difference between *The Plague*'s fictional format and the nonfictional, direct espousal of claims in, say, the Sartre selection; but they could also understand how *The Plague* matched up with the nonfictional *L'Homme révolté.* For instance, I correlated Tarrou's gradual disaffection from his rebellious comrades with *The Rebel*'s critique of revolutionary brutality and his aspiration to be an "innocent murderer" with *The Rebel*'s identically expressed aim (*Rebel* 105, 297). Furthermore, a number of students sensed Camus's intention in the selected passages (as in perhaps all his writing) to present not a systematic metaphysical theory but an informal and passionate "philosophy of life."

Comparison and discussion of philosophical positions.   The very design of the course, and the controversial issues in the textbook chosen, directed the class toward discussion and comparison of positions. The students approved of the course format in this regard, although many thought that the multiplicity of readings left insufficient time for discussion of interesting single selections like *The Plague.* My attempt to heighten comparison by contrasting Rieux and Tarrou's atheism with traditional Christianity only partially succeeded; there was surprisingly little student involvement during the class, and I had to explicate most of the relationships myself. Answers to examination questions, however, indicated some absorption of the comparison; and responses to the questionnaire claimed an understanding of the Paneloux versus Rieux-Tarrou parallelism. Many students also showed, through their examination responses, an understanding of the differences in terminology, scope, and content between Camus and Sartre, although some were rather blindly influenced by the editor's claim that Camus based his approach on "existentialist" freedom and self-creation.

Evaluation of philosophical positions.   Both the examination and the questionnaire indicated that students had been able to make some estimate of Camus and that this estimate was positive within the limitations imposed by their religious beliefs. In answering the examination question on atheism, most students saw Camus as more informed on and sympathetic to religion than were the other avowed atheists read, Sartre and Russell;[1] they also felt that Camus's humanitarianism was consistent with a Christian position. Questionnaire answers confirmed a grudging admiration for Rieux and Tarrou, because of their struggle against an overwhelming foe, their "saintly" devotion to fellow human beings, and their expression of the human spirit. Most students were repelled by the characters' atheism, but this negative feature had probably stimulated the students' reaction, and thus their evaluation, in the first place.

The other pertinent examination question—concerning Burton Porter's classification of existentialism, and therefore of *The Plague*, as taking a "metaphysical" position on "the nature of reality"—forced some student evaluation of the textbook editor. Some answered that Camus did have a metaphysics in his assumption of an indifferent godless nature, while others said he concentrated only on the human predicament.

Pedagogical Recommendations

The lecture-discussion method employed in Perspectives in Philosophy is not the only appropriate format for teaching *The Plague*. Other approaches might include dramatic reading, audiovisuals, and role playing (Rieux, Tarrou, and Paneloux, for instance?). Whatever format is adopted should, however, fit the personality and skills of the instructor. Also, no format should detract from or substitute for students' reading of the written word, which remains the primary mode of absorbing the novel. And, finally, one function of the instructor in any approach ought to be to provide background on the author, so that the work might be understood in an historical and literary context; such "contextualism" is an especially appropriate goal for an interdisciplinary humanities course.

In courses in French literature or the modern novel, it would seem inappropriate to read only short selections from *The Plague* rather than the whole work. A philosophy course, though, need not dwell on character and plot development (to whatever extent it might be present in *The Plague*[2]) but seeks primarily a novel's thought content, which can sometimes be found distilled in judiciously chosen passages. *The Plague* contains many such "moralizing" passages in which characters express their philosophical views, and the Porter selection exploited two of the most promising ones.

I would not insist that all instructors of *The Plague* adopt my requirements of quizzes, examinations, and term paper, since I realize that in other instructional hands less formal measures, such as role playing and discussion groups, could motivate reading, comparison, and evaluation by students. I do, however, believe in the weakness of human nature, and I did consider it imperative that students read the written text. The quiz motivated students to peruse the text and to understand its literal content, while the examination forced them to think comparatively about the content and to estimate it critically. The book report, which required that students read and organize an entire work, partially compensated for the brevity of class and reading time devoted to the selection.

A confirmation of my confidence in examinations was the students' performance when asked to deal with the "religious issue" in *The Plague*. As I have said, my classroom correlation of atheism and Christianity provoked little student response, while students seemed more prepared to confront Camus's atheism on the examination. A possible explanation is that they were not accustomed to having their own Christian religion regarded as a thought system, much less as an ideology in competition with other belief systems. By the time of the examination, they may have had occasion to become inured to this avenue of interpretation.

The Plague *as Philosophical Literature*

A work of literature has philosophical value only if it makes, illustrates, or implies philosophical claims. Characters in *The Plague* clearly take philosophical positions, and a composite philosophy of the novel as a whole can be constructed, and confirmed, through *L'Homme révolté*. Since the reading of *The Plague* in Perspectives in Philosophy was restricted to two short passages, I shall concentrate on these sections of the novel; fortunately, they happen to comprehend most of the work's principal themes.

The philosophical teaching of *The Plague* may be epitomized as follows. Humankind is plagued by suffering and death inflicted by nature and humans themselves; this plague is abetted by the indifference of ordinary people to its prospect and presence. Many adopt abstractions that help them avoid confrontation with the plague; a popular abstraction is the religious imputation of suffering to human guilt. Another abstraction is revolutionary ideology, which rationalizes its right to kill on a massive scale in order to combat injustice. The humane reaction to the plague shares with revolution an outrage at the injustice of evil but substitutes for revolutionary violence a sympathy and love for the plague's victims, leading to an attempt to forestall death and alleviate suffering. This attempt must be limited to a nonideological solution of the immediate human problems created by the plague, although given individuals might seek a personal purity in doing so.

Is the above really philosophy? It lacks important characteristics valued in the conventional Western philosophical tradition. Its concerns are quite narrow, containing no claims in epistemology or logic, for instance, and only the barest metaphysics (an indifferent nature without a God). There is no argumentation and no explicit concern for theoretical consistency. It has few links with major schools of contemporary philosophy; for one thing, despite Porter's claim, its status as existentialism is questionable, since it lacks two traits of that school—an overriding concern for human freedom and authenticity and the use of the phenomenological method.

Many of these limitations may, of course, be excused because *The Plague* is fiction and therefore of a genre in which elaborate arguments and theoretical pretensions are hardly appropriate. But the philosophy it does contain should not be sold short. Camus accurately critiques certain tenets of traditional Christianity, exposes the uncontrollable rationalization within political ideologies, and wisely calls for a moderate politics aimed toward finite problem solving rather than social transformation. In *The Plague* he is, as always, sensitive to the implications for practical living involved in given theoretical programs. While *The Plague*'s philosophy may be at most a "philosophy of life," a personal creed about the meaning of life and the way it should be lived, it includes, unlike most other life philosophies, accurate renditions and criticisms of competing viewpoints.

How effective is *The Plague* as an expression of this philosophy? It has been claimed that *The Plague* is Camus's most popular work (Thody, *Camus 1913–1960* 93), and in some ways this popularity is understandable. Students who did read the entire work were fascinated by the double allegory (once they became aware of the two levels of nonliteral interpretation) and were edified by the moral and humanitarian tone. The philosophical content of the novel was fairly easy to pick out, because of the many intellectual dialogues among characters and the many comments by the chronicler. But these advantages also present the dangers of homiletic moralizing and abstract allegorizing; to quote André Gide's hyperbole, "Good sentiments make bad literature" (Quilliot, *Sea* 152).

This ambivalent situation has been corroborated in my experience with teaching *The Plague* and *The Stranger*. Students reported that *The Plague*'s allegories had interested them and that its morality had been inspiring. But, whereas students in earlier courses had needed no special incentive to finish *The Stranger* and had eagerly discussed it, *The Plague* elicited neither of these reactions. My hypothesis is that students were somewhat put off by the frequent moralizing in *The Plague* and somewhat sedated by the novel's humanitarianism and by its critique of revolution, both of which are familiar themes in American culture. By contrast, Meursault in *The Stranger* had represented a fascinating alternative to moralism, both in his anesthetized hedonism before his arrest and in his subsequent attempt to raise himself by his own individualistic bootstraps.

The Plague is better ethics and politics than *The Stranger*, but the very superiority of its thought renders it less provocative. Perhaps *The Plague* would have turned out more provocative if Camus's conversion from his earlier individualism had not been so passionate and if he had not been so prone to preach his conversion through the mouths of his characters. But then, without passionate interest in ideas affecting life, Camus would not have been Camus.

NOTES

[1] This judgment is supported by Jean Onimus, *Albert Camus and Christianity*, 47.

[2] John Cruickshank (*Albert Camus* 172–74) discusses the weakness of character and plot in *The Plague*.

Crime and the Anarchist in *The Plague*

Robert R. Brock

The Plague is one in a series of twentieth-century French novels that I teach either in French as part of our B.A. program or in English as part of the humanities program. The reading of each novel is preceded by a general lecture on the author and his ideas. While the other authors in the group (Mauriac, Gide, Malraux, Robbe-Grillet) may be largely unknown to many of the students, most will have read some Camus, and so at the beginning of the Camus segment I ask them to describe his thinking. Their most common response is that he was an existentialist philosopher. I get some rather suspicious stares when I point out that he refused the label "existentialist" and that, instead of being a philosopher, since that word implies some sort of system, he was more of a moralist and, in my opinion, an anarchist as well. Their reaction stems from a misunderstanding of the term "anarchist," which, for Americans, conjures up comic-strip images of sinister men in long black cloaks carrying bombs with lighted fuses. It is my contention, however, that many elements of Camus's work, and the treatment of the criminal in particular, make more sense if examined in the light of French anarchist thought.

Two or three observations are in order at this point. First of all, although economic equality is of primary concern to the politically active anarchist, it is of no serious importance to Camus, who deals mainly with questions of individual liberty and responsibility. Second, although some terrorists call themselves anarchists, their penchant for violence is incompatible with basic French concepts of anarchism. Joseph Prudhon, the nineteenth-century theoretician and father of modern anarchist thought in France, used the word "anarchy" in the sense of its Greek root: an absence of authority or government. Although the connotation of "disorder" has been attached to the word in modern times, it is not part of the original meaning of the word. Prudhon believed that representative government, or any form of centrally directed government, should be abolished and that the people should govern themselves in what amounts to pure participatory democracy. Thus, in the absence of central authority, it is the duty of each person to participate both as an individual and as a committee member in the management of public affairs. Such participation must ensure not only the common good but also the total personal liberty of each member of the society. For that is the key idea: total personal liberty. This concept is the closest thing the anarchists have to a dogma. It is so strongly held that anarchists who are unable to accept any given decisions of their committees have the right to withdraw from the committees, without prejudice, and not to return until they can do so with a clear conscience. In case of conflict between personal liberty and the general welfare, anarchists believe that the general welfare will eventually prevail since, again in their opinion, human beings are self-perfectable. It is the belief in total personal liberty that prevents the true anarchist from indulging in violence since to do so would deprive others of their right to liberty, including the right to hold dissenting opinions.

With these concepts of personal liberty and duty in mind, I open the discussion of *The Plague* by examining Rambert, the Parisian journalist. Rambert is determined to leave Oran, even at the risk of spreading the plague, in order to rejoin the woman he loves. He asks Dr. Rieux if he is wrong in preferring his own happiness to all other considerations, in particular the general welfare of others. He is also worried that Rieux will inform the police of his intentions. Since Rambert could spread the disease that Rieux is trying to control, the doctor's seemingly irresponsible attitude may well seem incomprehensible to us. From an anarchist's standpoint, however, Rieux must state that Rambert is *not* wrong (note that he does not say that Rambert is right), because Rambert has an absolute right to his personal liberty. Moreover, Rieux cannot inform the police since he might thereby contribute to the suppression of Rambert's liberty and an anarchist simply cannot assume that responsibility. Rambert's dilemma, the conflict between his personal desires and the common good, is rather neatly resolved by his deciding to stay in Oran and join a nonofficial committee that is fighting the plague. At the same time, two anarchist principles have been demonstrated: Rambert has made the proper choice of the general welfare, and he has become a participant in public activities. A third principle has been demonstrated by Rieux's attitude: faith in one's fellows.

Nonetheless, the concept of total individual liberty does pose a problem: the potential abuse of that liberty. Since there is no anarchist dogma, it is impossible to think "wrong," as we saw with Rambert. It is possible, however, to act wrongly by depriving others of their liberty. Anarchist thinking holds that no one will be truly free until all are free, the ultimate goal of anarchism. To punish me by imprisoning me for acting improperly is to deprive me of my liberty. Since depriving me of my liberty is wrong, the very punishment of crime is a crime. It is for this reason that Camus, discussing judges in *The Rebel*, states that these representatives of "justice" have chosen crime for themselves when they punish others and that unless they can prove their own innocence, which is impossible, the prisons must be emptied. Although the anarchists believe that human beings are self-perfectable, the problem to be faced until that millennium arrives is what to do about those who fail to respect the liberty of others. Not surprisingly, anarchist writers do not dwell at great length on that subject.

Bakunin, a nineteenth-century Russian anarchist and disciple of Prudhon, states that criminal acts are to be considered a manifestation of an illness and that punishment is to be a cure rather than society's traditional reprisal. Maurice Joyeux, a contemporary French theoretician and, O paradox, a sometime candidate for the French presidency, simply states that human beings are not guilty, that is, not guilty of anything. According to Joyeux, individuals are the way they are either by chance or God's design, depending on one's personal beliefs. In either case, since they have not transgressed by choice, they are innocent and do not merit traditional punishment. Since they retain their right to total personal liberty, they have the right to refuse punishment. Indeed, Prudhon believed that criminals should agree to punishment only if they felt that it would benefit them. Criminals can refuse punishment by declaring that they no longer wish to be a part of their particular society or group. The group then has the right to exile them. With that in mind, the class is now asked to examine Cottard.

It is obvious early in *The Plague* that Cottard is a criminal. Clear indications include his distress at the prospect of having his botched suicide attempt reported to the police and his question to Dr. Rieux about whether the police have a right to arrest a person ill in a hospital. Even more interesting is his storming out of the tobacconist's shop after the woman's statement that "trash" like the commercial employee who had killed an Arab on the beach near Algiers should be thrown into prison. The commercial employee would seem to be Meursault from *The Stranger* (*L'Etranger*), who did shoot an Arab on a beach near Algiers. Since I believe that Camus has brought Meursault into the story, I feel that it is proper for me to review his case. I point out that Meursault, a European, was brought to trial for having shot an Arab who had pulled a knife on him in a land where, before World War II, Arabs had precious few rights. I add that, in my opinion, since the Arab had no family that we see and no friends at the trial and did not even have a name, he was not really a character but a pretext. That is, someone had to be sentenced to die to enable Camus to write a polemic against the death penalty. By ignoring the Arab and placing all the emphasis on Meursault, Camus has given us not a criminal but a victim, a victim of traditional justice. Cottard is treated in much the same manner. We do not know of what crime he stands accused; we know simply that it was not murder. Instead we see his anguish, his pathetic attempts to create a new personage for himself, and we note that while he is not particularly admirable, neither is he despicable. Moreover, once the gates of Oran are shut, Cottard is very effectively in exile with past crimes abolished and a chance to mend his ways.

Once the place and importance of Cottard are established, we examine Camus's use of the plague as a metaphor for World War II with its collective guilt (Paneloux's sermon), isolation, crematoriums, and so on. The next important discussion of crime and the anarchist viewpoint comes with Tarrou's confession. As in *The Stranger* we again have a prosecuting attorney, Tarrou's father, demanding the guillotine for an accused criminal, and again, there is not one word about the alleged crimes of this man Camus describes as a "frightened owl." In fact, Tarrou felt that the man was guilty but "of what crime is no matter." In reaction to that execution and the society that demanded it, Tarrou becomes a political activist, approving policies he knows will lead to the deaths of others. It is only later, while again witnessing an execution, that Tarrou is forced to recognize that he is no different from his father. Despite all the brave words about a perfect society where there will be no more killing, men have been sentenced to death and he has approved.

The plague is now a metaphor not only for passing the death sentence but also for approving the consequent deaths. It matters not whether the "dirty mouths stinking of plague" belong to the red robes or the revolutionaries. Tarrou sees them all as being plague bearers and refuses further association with those who, for good reasons or bad, bring death to others or justify their deaths. Since, in Tarrou's mind, all systems approve of at least some deaths for what are perceived to be good reasons and since Tarrou cannot approve of the taking of life under any circumstances, there can be only one logical solution: refuse all systems. That is, become an anarchist.

As the epidemic draws to a close, Cottard and Tarrou meet for the last time. Cottard is upset at the prospect of the quarantine's being lifted because it means his exile will be over and he will again be subject to arrest for his past crimes. He tells Tarrou that it would be great to be able to begin anew with a "clean sheet." But he had already been given that chance when the gates were first shut, and he had refused it. Not only did he deal in the black market, he had approved of the plague, saying that it suited him perfectly well, and had refused participation in the sanitary squads, the nonofficial committees formed by Tarrou. When two men, obviously plainclothesmen, ask him if his name is Cottard, he takes flight, later barricading himself in his room and firing on people in the street. If we read these pages carefully, we again note the anarchist mind at work. First of all, it is not possible for Cottard to be truly guilty of a crime. According to Tarrou, his only real crime is having approved of that which kills children and adults, and in one policeman's opinion, later echoed by Grand, he's gone mad. Second, when they take him alive, one of the officers strikes him in the face twice and then kicks him when he falls to the ground. This gratuitous brutality, more than a little reminiscent of the scene in *The Stranger* where the officer slaps Raymond Sintès, ensures that the reader will sympathize with Cottard and not with the police. Had they killed him in a shoot-out, they would have been acting in self-defense, and the reader's sympathies would have been with that most immediate and disliked symbol of authority, the police.

In all this, we see Cottard do but a single mean thing; he shoots a stray dog. The incident has no real importance in the story, and certainly no connection with anarchism, but it intrigues by its very gratuitousness. It is as though Camus were amusing himself by giving us a little puzzle to solve. Taking it in that vein, we note that the dog Cottard shoots is a spaniel and that there is at least one other spaniel in Camus's work: the one Salamano loses in *The Stranger* in another Algerian city, Algiers. I find a fair amount of rather grim humor in the description of the dog's wandering down the street and stopping to scratch its fleas, and even in the description of its grotesque death throes. As to why Camus would indulge in such a diversion, the answer is probably in the long discussion between Tarrou and Rieux: one cannot fight the plague all the time, one has to have a simple pleasure or two. Tarrou and Rieux go for a swim.

Tarrou has long since recognized that he is a plague bearer and has attempted to redeem himself. He will not be a part of a legal governing body, but he will organize an unofficial committee, the sanitary squads, to serve the common good. Where the government would use conscripts, Tarrou will accept only volunteers since participation will probably amount to a death sentence and one has the right to choose that only for one's self. The choice to serve is to be seen not as heroic but simply as necessary for the common good. Tarrou's actions concretize yet again the anarchist belief in the perfectability of humankind. That is, properly instructed and enlightened, men and women will become altruistic, preferring, like Rambert, the general welfare to their own personal well being.

As Dr. Rieux continues his rounds, he thinks not of his dead friend Tarrou but of Cottard and the fists smashing Cottard's face, because, as Camus notes, it is "harder to think of a guilty man than a dead one." But, in keeping with anarchist principles, there are no guilty characters in the book. At worst, Cottard is culpable of selfishness, hardly a real crime. And in this allegory of World War II, not only are the rats innocent of any wrongdoing, there is no evil genius to have unleashed them. Like Prudhon and Bakunin before him, Camus prefers to dwell on the positive aspects of human nature in its striving for a better world.

The Surgical Masque:
Representations of Medicine in Literature

Ailene S. Goodman

Peut-être, observaient les carnets, ne peut-on aboutir
qu'à des approximations de sainteté. Dans ce cas, il
faudrait se contenter d'un satanisme modeste et
charitable.

La Peste

Because I believe that a fusion of science and literature is desirable for both
science and literature majors, I have designed a seminar that focuses on the
motif of the doctor and culminates in Camus's *The Plague*. (The pivotal works
are listed and briefly discussed below.)

The plague is a difficult theme for intensive study. It is ugly, loathsome,
monstrous, unnatural (from the standpoint of healthy young students), violent; a recurring phenomenon throughout history and a continual backdrop
from the very beginning of known literature to the present. The effects of
plague are so devastating and so long-lasting that, though we have never
experienced the disease, we can still shudder at the force of Mercutio's curse
"A plague o' both your houses!" and we can understand why Barbara Tuchman's *A Distant Mirror: The Calamitous Fourteenth Century* (with its vivid
description of plague) can still be a best-seller.

The role of a devastating epidemic converts to political terms with very
little change of dress. Students can grasp the plague as political allegory
from numerous works such as Sophocles' *King Oedipus*, Thucydides' *The
Peloponnesian War* (and Thomas Hobbes's use of that work), William Lang-
land's *Piers the Ploughman*, Thomas Dekker's *The Seven Deadly Sins*, Daniel
Defoe's *A Journal of the Plague Year*, Romain Rolland's *Colas Breugnon
Burgundian* (ch. 7), and Ionesco's *Rhinoceros*. Camus's *The Plague* is the
gem of its kind. (For an interpretation of the genre among Camus's contem-
poraries, see Mavis Gallant.)

My course bears the same title as does this article. At the center of the
course stands the healer—wearing antiseptic mask and protective clothing—
exemplified by Camus's Dr. Bernard Rieux. (Camus's play, *State of Siege*,
published the year after *The Plague*, portrays in the classical roles of chorus,
Plague, and seer [medicus] the more subtle figures whom the class and I
will be examining in the novel.) The title of the course is inspired by Rieux,
who first appears emerging from his surgery, and by the theatrical form in

which allegorical types—such as "God, the physician" and "Evil, the destroyer of life"—perform. The role of the scientific practitioner in ethics, mythology, and social cataclysm is discussed through the various literary presentations. Among approaches are ancient, medieval, and modern satire; figurative (metaphoric) language; and thematic study (the social position and evaluation of the physician) in comedy as well as in tragedy. As an aid to concentrating on *The Plague* within this context, balanced readings and a selection of visual aids enable the student to tolerate what is a grotesque and exceedingly grim subject. Depending on their availability, four texts from the following five are required:

1. Ben Jonson, *The Alchemist.* (Alchemic tracts [see editions with prefaces and commentary by Henry E. Sigerist] written by the renowned medicomystic Paracelsus and his disciples will deepen an appreciation of Ben Jonson's astonishing comic genius.)

2. Molière, *The Imaginary Invalid.* (The doctor from the point of view of the patient. Along with the very funny plays of Molière [see also his *The Flying Doctor* and *The Doctor in Spite of Himself*], readings in John Donne's poetry, devotions, and sermons on illness, in metaphor and in fact, will increase a student's understanding of the ethical and social concepts satirized here.)

3. Goethe, *Faust.* (The dilemma of the heretic; the diabolical *Doppelgänger*. For students of psychotherapy and related disciplines, clinical and literary studies on the double motif [see Rank] will stimulate informed discussion of self-awareness in Goethe's [and Marlowe's] Doctor Faustus and in Camus's Dr. Rieux.)

4. Arthur Schnitzler, *Professor [Doctor] Bernhardi.* (The probings and soul searchings of a Jewish physician as subject and object of real and metaphorical constraint; the politics and social structure of medicine. Compare to the layers of meaning in Camus's Paneloux, Rieux, and Tarrou.)

5. Camus, *The Plague.* (The ancient healer-magician-priest concept of the *medicus.* Doctor Vickery in Joyce Carol Oates's *Son of the Morning,* even sampled in a brief excerpt, will do much to clarify this concept.)

In addition to these texts, supplementary selected requisite texts (see app. A) constitute the material for oral book reports assigned to individuals (or to small groups or to the whole class if time and the load in other classes permit) at the teacher's discretion. These book reports, photocopied and distributed to all, are considered required reading and are discussed in class as well as included on exams. Students with particular research interests may also be assigned to report on certain works listed in appendix B.

As dealt with by scholars in many disciplines—among them psychology, public health, and anthropology—the symbolism of medicine might illuminate the history of civilization from many angles. "Since ancient times, sickness has been perceived as a struggle between the patient and the demons of disease in which the aid of the gods was sought" (Jayne 104). Sickness and health are the essence of *The Plague*. How these elements are represented proves the creative genius of Camus.

The Myth of the Healer

Science has traditionally seemed to be a kind of magic; the oldest myths portray the soft light of the moon as healer, the moon deity as magician, priest, counselor, and physician. Often, too, in mythology, the heavenly healer is the sun, the enlightener, with its power to warm people and to bring the crops they plant to fruition. Against these usually benign images are the destructive forces: storms, winter, epidemics. The daily rising of the sun signals the healer's victory in the battle, just as the setting of the sun indicates a new onslaught by the enemy.

Similarly, the representation of the plague as the power of demons is rooted in prehistory. The devil, for example, may be pictured wearing the mask of the plague (or, as in Camus's drama *The State of Siege*, the personified plague may appear in the figurative mask of the devil). In an Oriental legend to which Camus alludes ("the genius of plague" [*The Plague*, Mod. Lib. Coll. ed. 86]), exorcism of the demons of plague suggests a psychological release bred of desperation. The following is from E. T. C. Werner, *Myths and Legends of China* (151):

> The Grand Master of the Taoists was trying to stay the ravages of a pestilence, but he could not conquer the devils which caused it. Under these circumstances he appealed to [The Three Musical Brothers] and asked them their advice as to what course to adopt. T'ien Yüan-shuai had a large boat built, called "Spirit-boat." He assembled in it a million spirits, and ordered them to beat drums. On hearing this tumult all the demons of the town came out to listen. T'ien Yüan-shuai, seizing the opportunity, captured them all and, with the help of the Grand Master, expelled them from the town.

In many eras and many cultures, health is the good, illness the evil. Health and illness have been viewed as the benevolent and malevolent adversaries:

the good (or "god") represents order, or divine harmony; the evil (or "pest" or "plague" in the broadest sense of the words) represents disorder, a diseased society, a diseased morality. The victim is the "patient," who "suffers"—bears or endures—the battle raging within the physical body, or metaphorical "state."

In daily contact with the inexplicable cycle of worldly life and death, the physician is viewed as omniscient, a kind of seer, closely associated with health and illness, familiar enough with magic to be able to contend with the powers of evil. And so the healer image is said to function not only in the realm of heaven but also in the realm of hell. Somewhere between the divine and the demonic worlds, the figure of the doctor perches, a personification of godliness when healing is successful, a reminder of damnation when healing fails.

This view of the doctor is best limned in the ancient poetry of Ovid's *Metamorphoses*. In this episodic poem (pp. 384–88 in Humphries; see app. A), Aesculapius, whose epithets include "son of Apollo" and "god of medicine," is called to Rome to avert "a deadly pestilence":

> . . . He spoke, or seemed to, calmly:
> "Be not afraid; I shall come, and leave my statues,
> But see this serpent, as it twines around
> The rod I carry: mark it well, and learn it,
> For I shall be this serpent, only larger,
> Like a celestial presence." (bk. 15, lines 658–63)

Looped and coiled on the mast of the ship, Aesculapius, like a mythic Eastern dragon, dazzling in golden reptile scales, causes the people to shudder in awe and to worship at his shrine, until at last,

> [The god of medicine] had entered Rome, the capital
>   of the world,
> And climbed the mast, and swung his head about
> As if to seek his proper habitation . . .
> . . . .
>   Here the serpent-son,
> Apollo's offspring, came to land, put on
> His heavenly form again, and to the people
> Brought health and end of mourning. (736–38, 741–44)

In analyzing the role of Camus's Dr. Rieux, the teacher can use the ambivalent image of god and serpent, for it embodies the two sides of human nature. The "plague" is tyrannical, insidious, and oddly attractive—like a serpent. The "true healer" is expected to act as a good angel, superhuman and omniscient—like a god. Translated into theatrical terms, a doctor's daily routine might be called "The Surgical Masque," for it enacts an ancient role, performed in ritual costume. Reflecting roots in antiquity, like the professorial stock character of commedia dell'arte, the practitioner of the healing arts today still appears "abstract" (the word is Camus's: *The Plague* 81) in prophylactic coat and cap and gloves, with facial features inscrutable behind an antiseptic, or "surgical," mask.

In Camus the three elements initially are presented as discrete: the Victim, the Plague, and the Healer. Curiously, however, they are often entangled—until in the last lines of the book, they cohere, and the plague bides its time "for the bane and enlightening of men." "Bane"-"enlightening": we have seen a similar phrase before: "benevolent"-"diabolism"—but used to describe not the plague but the healer—and will come to this oddity presently. Reading Camus's allegory, one is reminded of the merged identity of Ovid's Aesculapius: on the one hand, an earthly physician, metamorphosed as a serpent—archaic symbol of the shadowed world of procreation and decay underneath the green ground of vegetation; on the other hand, a dazzling deity—symbol of warm sunshine and (usually) celestial compassion, harmony or (in *The Plague* 230) "peace." Struggling to assist Rieux, whom he values among the "true healers" (230), Tarrou fuses the opposites—Victim and Plague—from an evocative polarity; as he states in the quotation at the head of this essay, "Perhaps . . . we can only reach approximations of sainthood. In which case we must make shift with a mild, benevolent diabolism" (248).

"Mild, benevolent diabolism": much can be made of this most jolting figure, as of other such contrastive expressions that occur throughout the book. (Already mentioned is the plague as "bane"-"enlightening," for example. On the first page, again, "extraordinary" events were "out of place" in "ordinary" Oran; the town appears "grafted" [5] onto the landscape.) Is Tarrou's phrase, "mild, benevolent diabolism," merely a pretentious oxymoron, or is it the pith of Camus's thesis—the reason Camus selected Rieux, and not one of the others, to be the author's ombudsman? Reflections of health and illness converge and diverge from one character to the next, and even within one character. The priest, Father Paneloux, in his first plague sermon, instructs plague sufferers to believe his message of comfort, "And God would see to the rest" (91). But the clear argument is diffused when, a few chapters later, Rieux, "his face still in shadow," counters (to Tarrou) that "if he [Rieux] believed in an all-powerful God he would cease curing the sick and leave that to Him."

"I now can picture what this plague must mean for you," Tarrou tells his hero. "Yes. A never ending defeat," Rieux rejoins (118). But, of course, like the face of Apollo the sun god, Rieux's face does not remain "in shadow," and in the bright light of his actions, the pessimistic words are denied. How far apart are Paneloux and Rieux, in word and deed? Students will quote instances of eloquence and humility in both their natures, from the poignant scenes of the torturing pain suffered by M. Othon's little child and of the racking death of Father Paneloux. The theological conversations between them, as between Tarrou and Rieux, recall a philosophical work by the gentle Baroque physician Thomas Browne, whose name during his lifetime was on Rome's "condemned" list for his seeming atheism. In defense of his ethics, Browne wrote the beautiful book called *Religio Medici: A Doctor's Religion* (see app. A): "God is merciful unto all. . . . To say he punisheth none in this world is no absurdity" (64). "Charity . . . is the love of God, for whom wee love our neighbour: for this I thinke is charity, to love God for himselfe, and our neighbour for God" (92). "Blesse mee in this life with but the peace of my conscience . . ." (93). In an exquisite segment from *The Plague*, Rieux too feels compelled to defend himself and define his creed. (See the next to last paragraph of the novel.) What *does* a doctor believe of him- or herself? What are the plague's effects on Rieux's wife? Rieux's mother? Paneloux? Tarrou? Rieux? Dr. Richard? Dr. Castel? For them, what is "a doctor's religion"?

The dilemma Rieux faces is encapsulized by two instances from Camus's novel. The backdrop for the first is the fatigue that plague workers are experiencing, manifested not only in their indifference to the agony they constantly witness and to any hope of a "decisive battle" or "armistice" but also in indifference to their own personal need to take adequate precautions against exposure to the infection (169). The implication is that this indifference is as pernicious as the bacterial infection. Can steeling oneself against pity lead to pitilessness? Rieux confesses to Grand his sense of negligence about his wife. Had she been with him he might have helped her recover; as it is, loneliness surely depresses her and impedes her progress.

The second instance is another confession of divided loyalties; for his self-sacrifice, Rieux is conscious not of the gratitude but of the hatred of those he has served. Where once his patients "welcomed [him] as a savior" (173), he realizes that he now is identified with the scourge he is fighting. "You haven't a heart," the families of the plague-stricken accuse him, as he arrives, accompanied by armed police, to take away their loved ones. Official authorities have decreed, on his persuasion, that plague victims and suspected carriers be isolated, at gunpoint when there is resistance. Doors are bolted against his law-enforcing arm, as if against, indeed, the folkloric "Grim Reaper," death, who with a vicious scythe cuts down tender flowers at the height of their bloom. (See Forster 83.) The growing callousness of the exhausted medical teams, and what is perceived by many as Rieux's dictatorial inhumanity, is the bitter reward of the hero. Plague evacuees are ordered to isolation centers given over to victims' care and restraint. Workers masked in prophylaxis respond woodenly to the call of duty. Exemplified by M. Othon, those thus removed from their homes suffer a kind of martyrdom that Camus (with literary precedent—see app. A, Donne) compares to solitary confinement in prison. A paradoxical social situation exists in which their very "exile" draws victims to huddle together in their isolation, terrorized both by the tyrannical plague and by the tyrannical healer. It is the age-old question that concerns Rieux—whether he, as cure, is worse than the disease. "To fight abstraction you must have something of it in your own make-up," Rieux has decided (83).

The pervasiveness in legend of this kind of Faustian ambivalence offers a clue to Rieux's strength, which in turn is the strength of the novel. A story of "Chief Pestilence" told by René Girard in his book *Violence and the Sacred* may clarify for students the challenge to Rieux's integrity. Chief Pestilence is akin to Camus's despotic plague (an "abstraction" in *The Plague*, a lordly personification in *State of Siege*). For us, the point of the legend is the duplicitous character of the healer figure; that is, he is simultaneously both cure and disease. According to Girard's segment from the lore of the Tsimshian, a native American nation of the Canadian Pacific coast (244), a young man has been horribly mutilated. Desiring only death, he journeys to the land of Chief Pestilence, who is "Master of Deformities." Like Camus's plague, Chief Pestilence wields a destructive magnetism over his subjects, who are outwardly monstrous, inwardly violent and cruel. The young man resists the easier course, which would be to join forces with values he detests. Lest he become the same as they, the young man carefully ignores the tribesmen. Chief Pestilence agrees to cure him, but at a terrible cost, for he must acquiesce to being boiled down to bare bones and then refleshed. Against the alternative of becoming a vassal of a monstrous presence, the young man steadfastly chooses the cure. Chief Pestilence restores him to his former beauty, and the young man departs. The hideousness of the grim choice appalls us. Danger is in the cure and in the disease.

Echoes of the theme resound throughout *The Plague*; Tarrou's apt phrase "mild, benevolent diabolism" is, after all, inherent in every healer epic, including Camus's. Archetypes, such as the drastic "Chief Pestilence" myth, abound. Students will find many more, but the teacher may begin with these three other examples: (1) In ancient Egyptian lore, the goddess Isis is portrayed as a healer. Yet to obtain her extraordinary magical powers, she had first to cause the destruction of Rā, her forerunner, the sun god—and then cure him. (2) In Homer's *Iliad*, Apollo inflicts pestilence before he becomes the healer. (3) In the Bible, God allows the sufferings of Job and then cures him. Within these surroundings, Camus's novel places Rieux on the divine side of human behavior. But, like the fathomless faces of the Roman god

Janus, the gods may be highly ambivalent, and Dr. Rieux too is complex. Immersed in the plague epidemic, Rieux must not dissolve in feelings of pity. Thus literally costumed in prophylaxis and wearing the mask of his profession, which face does he turn? when? and to whom? This is the doctor's dilemma, which Camus's *The Plague*, on many levels, so cogently explores.

The Healer's Dilemma

A dilemma, however, by its very nature, offers the possibility for humor as well as for horror, and Camus, with his playwright's superb sense of timing, has introduced humor into the novel at several points that students will readily discover. In a series of amusing vignettes, for example, the municipal office clerk, Joseph Grand, tries to compose a masterpiece, never getting beyond the first sentence, which recurs as a leitmotif. In Grand's principal image, one cannot help being reminded of the Bible's most dreaded config-uration: The "Four Horsemen of the Apocalypse"—invasion, civil strife, famine, and plague—from the Revelations of Saint John. It cannot be co-incidence that from this most ghastly pictorial symbol of pestilence and hell, Grand has derived an elegant horsewoman riding down a flower-strewn avenue. Out of the nightmarish fantasy of those biblical internecine horse-men comes this absurdly incongruous creature. Grand's own private bat-tle with plague completes the picture; indeed, the apocalyptic equestrian almost triumphs, but Grand's miraculous recovery deprives the specter of its winnings.

Graphics abound to illustrate the horseman motif: Pieter Brueghel's oil painting *The Triumph of Death* is one; Barbara Tuchman's *A Distant Mirror* describes others (124, 628n). For all its ghastly horror, this particular motif has been satirized, parodied, and caricatured as if it were the funniest idea in the world. The teacher can make the most of this fact, by showing students how Camus crafts comic interludes that contrast with the scene—as truth contrasts with hypocrisy. It is a good opportunity to point out that some of the grimmest of medical lore has been masterfully used in literature to create what one editor has described to me as a persiflage of curative treatment. Aristophanes, Plautus, Rabelais, Ben Jonson, Montaigne, and Molière are only a few of the literati in the "medicine in literature" area. (See app. A and B.) A class may enjoy the assignment of devising its own reading list of the "healing arts" masquerade.

In sum, the mask is an insistent motif recurring in *The Plague*. Like the smiling and frowning faces of classical comedy and tragedy, the mask both obscures and heightens truth. The ancient word for "actor" on the Greek stage is akin to "hypocrite," and "hypocrisy" still conveys a two-faced image. The mask is featured in carnivals, and it is featured in religious ceremonies.

It mellows, and it exaggerates. It is awesome, and it is funny. In the most poignant scene of *The Plague*, the death of M. Othon's child, the joyous little body of childhood displays a death mask (194). In a grotesque mimicry of offstage fever, the Orpheus and Euridice scene, "plague [stands] on the stage in the guise of a disarticulated mummer" (180). Finally, in a terrible "Don Juan"–like irony, the face behind the medical mask is inscrutably "abstract," in the scene when Tarrou, Rambert, and Rieux wear "sterile masks of cotton-wool," so that "Whenever any of them spoke through the mask, the muslin bulged and grew moist over the lips. This gave a sort of unreality to the conversation; it was like a colloquy of statues" (187). In each of these three instances, there is a fearsome contrast between holy silence and diabolical scream; between operatic sound and dyslalia—and then the cries of dismay of the audience as in a *danse macabre* stampeding in terror to the exit; between impotent silence and muffled confidence. In scene after scene, figure after figure, the mask provides protection between the performer's vulnerability and the capacity to speak. As Mavis Gallant, describing the role of writers during the occupation, observes, "troubled times" gave rise to "every form of ambiguity human conduct can devise." The prophylactic surgical mask over the noses and mouths of medical teams reacting to the tyrannical plague afforded precisely the ambiguity needed by Camus's "impartial observer" (271).

The 1656 engraving by Paulus Fürst, *Der Doctor Schnabel von Rom: Pestarzt in einer Schutzkleidung*, and similar pictures with which Camus was acquainted do much to explain to a student the physician's mask. Behind the "bird's beak" were aromatic mixtures through which the wearer breathed to guard against infection. The wand was used partly to avoid touching the patient. The long academic gown and cap were symbols of social prestige as well as useful and protective overclothes. The idea of a mask was furthered by protective glasses. Prophylactic gloves completed the image of impersonal social contact. Such circulars as this one were widely recognized as satire. For though legitimate circulars were intended to acquaint the "plague doctor" with hygienic measures, the guise clearly evoked hallucinations of the devil in the minds of feverish sufferers. The Jesuit priest and plague doctor Hippolytus Guarinonius gently parodied the problem in an amusing bit of poetic doggerel (1652):

> Three faces has the doctor: angel, demigod, and devil. An angel when he first appears; demigod when he helps us out of danger; but a devil straight from Hell when he holds out his hand for his fee.   (qtd. in Dörrer 101, trans. mine)

On completing *The Plague*, Camus reworked the subject into drama, *L'Etat de siège*. In one scene (54, Fr. ed.; 157, Eng. ed.; see app. A) a medical student, Diego, pushes through the terrified crowd that superstitiously hears the wings of "death" in the howling wind and sees dire prophecies of plague in fiery comets. Camus's stage directions specify the plague doctor's mask and note the fear this mild young lover incongruously arouses:

> [Victoria] court à une extrémité de la scène et se heurte à Diégo qui porte le masque de médecins de la peste. Elle recule, poussant un cri. Diégo (doucement): "Je te fais donc si peur, Victoria?"

> She runs to the far end of the stage and collides with Diego, who is wearing the mask of the plague doctors. She recoils, gasping. Diego (gently): "Do I frighten you so much, Victoria?"

APPENDIX A

*Axis text; **supplementary requisite; supplementary optional

Abraham à Sancta Clara, sermons (trans. in Nohl; see app. B).

Bible, Book of Job.**

Boccaccio, *Decameron*, introd. plus one story.**

Thomas Browne, *Religio Medici*, in vol. 1 of *Works*, ed. Geoffrey Keynes (Chicago: Univ. of Chicago Press, 1964).

Albert Camus, *Notebooks*, trans. Justin O'Brien (New York: Knopf, 1965) **; see esp. vol. 2, notebook 4.

——, *The Plague*, trans. Stuart Gilbert (New York: Modern Library College Editions).*

——, *La Peste* (Paris: Gallimard, 1947).

——, *State of Siege*, in *Caligula and Three Other Plays*, trans. Stuart Gilbert (New York: Knopf, 1958), 135–232.*

——, *L'État de siège* (Paris: Gallimard, 1948).

Daniel Defoe, *A Journal of the Plague Year.***

Thomas Dekker, *The Wonderful Year.*

John Donne, *Devotions upon Emergent Occasions* nos. 1, 4, 5, 6, 12, 17; "The Plague Sermon"; and poem "Hymn to God, My God, in My Sickness."**

Goethe, *Faust* (pt. 1).*

Homer, *The Iliad.*

Eugene Ionesco, *Rhinoceros.*

Ben Jonson, *The Alchemist.**

Lucretius, *De Rerum Natura* (*The Way Things Are*), trans. Rolfe Humphries (Bloomington: Indiana Univ. Press, 1968), bk. 5, lines 52–411; bk. 6, lines 1042–1277.

Alessandro Manzoni, *The Betrothed* (*I Promessi Sposi*), Harvard Classics, vol. 21 (New York: Collier, 1909), chs. 31–37.**

Molière, *The Imaginary Invalid.**

Montaigne, *Essays*, trans. Charles Cotton (London: printed for the Navarre Soc., 1923), vol. 4, bk. 2, ch. 37, "Resemblance of Children to the Fathers."**

Joyce Carol Oates, *Son of the Morning* (New York: Vanguard, 1978).

Ovid, *Metamorphoses*, trans. Rolfe Humphries (Bloomington: Indiana Univ. Press, 1964).

Paracelsus, any available works, trans. and ed. Henry E. Sigerist.

Petrarch, poems to "Laura."

Procopius, *History of the Wars*, trans. H. B. Dewing (London: Heinemann, 1961), introd., vol. 1, pp. vii–xiii; vol. 2, ch. 22–23, pp. 453–71.

Rabelais, *Gargantua* and *Pantagruel* (London: Everyman-Dent, 1946), vol. 1, ch. 32, "How Pantagruel Covered a Whole Army with His Tongue . . ."**

Romain Rolland, *Colas Breugnon Burgundian*, ch. 7.

Arthur Schnitzler, *Professor Bernhardi.**

Sophocles, *King Oedipus.***

"There is a Reaper, His Name is Death," song, in Leonard Forster, ed., 83 (see app. B for full reference).*

Thucydides, *The Peloponnesian War*, "The Plague of Athens."

APPENDIX B: REFERENCES

(For full citations, see Works Cited)

Auerbach, Erich. *Mimesis.* "The World in Pantagruel's Mouth," 262–84.

Brée, Germaine. *Camus.* "Heroes of Our Time: *The Plague*," 118–30; "Camus and His Time," 3–11; "Algerian Summer, 1913–1932," 12–20.

Cipolla, Carlo M. *Faith, Reason and the Plague in Seventeenth-Century Tuscany.* Ch. 1.

Crawfurd, Raymond. *Plague and Pestilence in Literature and Art.*

Forster, Leonard, ed. *The Penguin Book of German Verse.*

Gallant, Mavis. "What Did Sartre Do during the Occupation?"

Girard, René. *Violence and the Sacred.*

Goodman, Ailene S. *Explorations of a Baroque Motif: The Plague in Selected Seventeenth-Century English and German Literature.*

———. "The Surgical Mask in Literature."

Jayne, Walter Addison. *The Healing Gods of Ancient Civilizations.*

Landa, Louis, introd. to Daniel Defoe, *A Journal of the Plague Year.*

Lottman, Herbert R. *Albert Camus: A Biography.*

Nohl, Johannes. *The Black Death.* See esp. "The Aspect of the Plague," 2–50, with excerpts from Abraham à Sancta Clara.

Ober, William B. and Nabil Alloush. "The Plague at Granada, 1348–1349: Ibn Al-Khatib and Ideas of Contagion."

O'Brien, Conor Cruise. *Albert Camus of Europe and Africa.*

Parry, Adam. "The Language of Thucydides' Description of the Plague."

Rank, Otto. *The Double.*

Shrewsbury, J. F. D. *A History of Bubonic Plague in the British Isles.*

Sigerist, Henry E. Alchemic works; editions and translations of Paracelsus' writings.

Tharpe, Jac, ed. *Art and Ethics: A Collection of Essays on Percy.*

Thomas, Lewis. "The Art of Teaching Science."

Thorndike, Lynn. *A History of Magic and Experimental Science.*

Tuchman, Barbara. *A Distant Mirror: The Calamitous Fourteenth Century.*

Werner, E. T. C. *Myths and Legends of China.*

TEACHING THE HISTORICAL, BIOGRAPHICAL, AND GEOGRAPHICAL CONTEXTS

Teaching the Historical Context of *The Plague*

Allen Thiher

In teaching courses on modern French fiction to advanced undergraduates and graduate students, I have usually arranged the course readings to follow the historical unfolding of the production of the works. I follow this historical order not out of any fetishistic respect for chronology but from a respect for the capacity of a historical framework to solicit and produce meanings in a text. Sometimes the referential dimension of a novel can only produce meaning when an appropriate historical or extratextual context is given to the work. But a historical framework does not just involve the relation between the novel and events in the world. It also involves the novel's relation to a history of literary works that have preceded the novel and to which the novel makes direct or indirect reference.

The historical context of *The Plague* is formed by the intersection of the many works with which Camus's novel maintains a dialogue—works of Sterne,

Melville, Nietzsche, Kafka, Dostoevsky, and much of French fiction of the two decades preceding publication of *The Plague*—and the political events that characterize French and European history in the twentieth century, especially the Nazi conquest of Europe and, later, the revelation of the mass trials and murders in Stalinist Russia. Or, as Camus would present it in his companion essay *The Rebel*, the historical context for *The Plague* is given by the development of the metaphysics of the absurd and the practical consequences of the belief in the absurd within the political history of the Western world. In contemporary history the absurd, the refusal of the belief in any transcendental absolutes, has, according to Camus, resulted in irrational and rational terrorisms, as embodied in the Nazi and the communist versions of the supremacy of state power.

This political reading demands that one enlarge the scope of what is often the focus of a literature course. Teaching strategies demand, moreover, that one approach an understanding of Camus's novel through a series of precise choices of readings that generate coherence for the entire course. My experience with these choices for a course on modern French fiction may be of some use to others, both teachers and students. Especially useful might be to consider how Camus's work marks what I consider a key moment in the history of French literature and thought. To establish the political and social outlines of this history I first ask students to read a history of modern France. Today's students (and perhaps yesterday's) tend to have only the most rudimentary notions about history. I find it most economical to have them read the history on their own, since I do not wish to spend class time lecturing on the subject. Occasion for historical explanation and interpretation, of course, arises in class. Every history text has its limitations. The essential thing initially is to provide students with the received facts about history—without too much concern for interpretation—that all French readers have at their command when they open a novel. For history is part of the referential dimension of language, and mastery of French entails mastery of a world of reference that is always present even if it is taken for granted by a reader who is fluent in the language.

The historical context provided by the literary works with which *The Plague* maintains relations involves the teacher's choice and the reader's experience. To create this context I divide my course into three historical "moments": first, that of modernist experimentation; second, the moment of the encounter with the absurd; and finally, the contemporary search for various forms of writing or *écriture*. In the first part we read writers such as Proust, Gide, and Colette. Many of their works, often in the form of quasi-autobiographical explorations of the self, seek to justify existence through art. This justification of life disappears in the course's second "moment." In this part, covering works from the 1930s through *The Plague*, I use the

absurd as an organizing theme to examine novels and stories reflecting what
Camus perceived as the central philosophical problem of the twentieth century. To explore the theme of the absurd, students read Céline, Malraux,
Sartre, and finally Camus. The coherence in this part is, I admit, largely
afforded by reading the works in a Camusian perspective, which comes to
a logical conclusion with *The Plague* and its critique of the absurd. *The
Plague* also orients students toward those later works that have given up the
political and ethical concerns at the heart of Camus's novel. In the third
"moment," texts by writers such as Beckett, Robbe-Grillet, Pinget, Saur-
raute, and Duras, though often imbued with a sense of the absurd, represent
a brave, new world that seems somehow on the other side of Camus. Camus
sets forth a humanist scale by which I invite students to measure these
contemporary writers. (And, in a spirit of impartiality, I invite students to
use Robbe-Grillet's essays as a nonhumanist scale by which to judge Camus.)

It is the second moment of this course that concerns us most here. Within
the historical context of the thirties and forties—a time of world depression,
the rise of fascism, and the spread of revolutionary hopes—the student must
make sense of novels that share the vision of a world bereft of meaning.
Earlier modernist works often make this assumption but do not celebrate
the absurd as the central feature of the world they present. Céline's *Journey
to the End of the Night* (1932) most clearly marks the eruption of a hopeless
vision of the absurd into French literary consciousness. Céline's parodistic
exploration of the self and of time past, an inversion of modernist aesthetics,
eventually demonstrates that madness has always been the essence of existence. Though Camus was not concerned with Céline specifically, Céline
offers a test case for Camus's reading of modern history, especially Camus's

belief that writers or intellectuals who accept the absurd often end up being
terrorists. Céline did become a protofascist later in the thirties. In contrast
to Céline is the Malraux of the thirties. His *Man's Fate* also embraces the
absurd as the fundamental category of existence but strives to overcome it
through the "viril fraternity" found in communist revolution. Céline's and
Malraux's novels bring up several political themes that stand behind *The
Plague*. They open up onto the thirties' world of jobless workers and fascist
uprisings and the importance of revolutionary movements in those distant
lands, such as Malraux's China, that would become the major features of
our political maps today. Malraux's novel, I might add, does necessitate
some lecturing, for I have yet to find the convenient source that would
quickly fill in all the gaps in students' knowledge of modern Chinese history.

Sartre's *Nausea* or the stories in *The Wall* can complete the literary historical background needed for reading *The Plague*. A photocopy of Camus's
reviews of *Nausea* and *The Wall*, found in the Pléiade edition of his *Essais*
(1417–22), can quickly show how these works, with their view of the absurd

as the total contingency of existence influenced Camus. *Nausea*, in particular, prompted Camus to think about the necessity of going beyond the absurd through something other than the curiously modernist attempt, at the end of the book, to have Roquentin justify existence by writing a novel—and this after Sartre's savage parody of modernist aesthetics throughout *Nausea*. *The Wall* also presents stories that tie Sartre's reflections on the absurd to the unfolding political history of Europe. "The Wall," for instance, shows a kind of absurdist paralysis of thought that parallels thinking about revolution throughout the thirties (the story narrates the discovery of the absurd by a revolutionary in the Spanish Civil War), whereas other stories set forth sketches of human conduct that illustrate the absurd in concrete existential terms, the final story showing how the absurd informs the genesis of a young fascist. In varying ways, then, the works by these three writers present an axiomatic acceptance of the absurd, of that nihilistic belief in the absurd that Camus felt to have its most radical historical consequences when it erupted in the form of the Nazi Occupation of France in 1940. For the Nazis, in their perverted way, sought to overcome nihilism by glorifying it.

In more advanced courses the teacher might wish to enlarge the students' perspective on *The Plague* by encouraging them to pursue other lines of reading, for the work is embedded in an extensive intertextual history. For example, Camus opens the work with a quotation from Defoe. The student with a comparative bent might turn to *A Journal of the Plague Year* not only for a literary "source" for Camus's description of the plague but especially for a primary example of the realist writing, grounded in an empiricist understanding of truth, that Camus adopts as part of his refusal of the abstract writings of system builders. For these systems, he believed, are all too often rationalizations of the forms of tyranny that contemporary history abounds in. Melville's *Moby-Dick* offers a parallel for its exploration of the way an open allegory can be written to endow a novel with a moral significance going beyond any given historical situation: the novel becomes a guide for interpreting history both past and future. According to Camus's own writings, works by Kafka and Dostoevsky exemplify meditations on the literary embodiment of the absurd that precede the more narrow historical context of the thirties. And with regard to philosophical texts, the capable student could be invited to compare Camus's thought and Nietzsche's reflections on nihilism, in such works as *Beyond Good and Evil*, *The Genealogy of Morals*, or especially the notes collected under the title *The Will to Power*. Such explorations of the history of Western literature and philosophy will of course be limited by the students' time and talents. But in any case readers should be aware that *The Plague* is situated in a broad context of intellectual and literary history that, in Camus's review, eventuated in the most important historical realities of the twentieth century: the glorification of the state in the rise of fascism and the perversion of utopian socialism that brought about the modern forms of communist tyranny.

These two historical forms of terrorism, as Camus calls them in *The Rebel*, impinged directly on life in France, and an understanding of both is necessary to grasp one aspect of the referential dimension of *The Plague*. As an open allegory, *The Plague* could be read without reference to Hitler's extermination of the Jews or to Stalin's purge trials. But *The Plague* is a novel about history, and to exclude these historical events from its field of reference would be a futile exercise. Rather, the most sensible reading is to see first how the novel works with regard to these monumental historical events. Then one can invite students to find other historical moments into which *The Plague* might offer insight or to imagine moments that might arise in the students' own experiences.

Most immediately *The Plague* appears to demand some knowledge of the French intellectual and political scene before and during the Occupation years of 1940–44. Though Camus had begun thinking of the plague as a symbol before these years and rewrote the novel in large part after the liberation, the Occupation years and their extraordinary history do seem to provide the first test case for finding a referential use for this allegory. After students have become familiar with this period, they are in fact more than eager to "apply" the novel to the historical facts at their command, for, at all levels of reading, these facts do illuminate what is taking place in the novel (and vice versa). But, before turning to a discussion of some of the relations that one can discern between the novel and the Occupation, I would offer the following caveat. Situating this or any other novel in historical context demands a certain sophistication, and students should be discouraged from reductionist readings that eliminate the work's more general meanings. On the most general level *The Plague* can offer insight into nearly any historical experience. The plague is not, therefore, the symbol of Nazi troops, or whatever the students first grasp as a possible referent for the novel's central allegorical figure. The teacher must make certain that students read the work as an exploration of a structure for interpreting historical experience, not simply as a thinly veiled univocal symbolic representation. For the same reason I hesitate to recommend biographies of Camus to students. It is all too easy for them to arrive at a simplistic reduction of the allegory whereby Rieux equals Camus, and Camus's isolation in southern France during part of the Occupation, for example, then "explains" the theme of exile expounded by Rieux. It is far more profitable for students to reflect on the public history of France's conflicts and defeat, or on the inconceivable but real existence of fascism, than to meditate on Camus's love life.

With this warning in mind, the teacher can guide students toward a kind of analogical reading that shows how *The Plague* is rooted in various ways in the real. The utterly surprising sudden defeat of the French and British armies in 1940 provides a model for the sudden spread of the plague. Perhaps no one is ever prepared for the total destruction of normal order and for the occurrence of the impossible. In this regard the inexplicable springtime victory of the plague bacillus parallels France's collapse in a few weeks at the hands of a motorized German army that seemingly nothing in Europe could stop. This army arrived in a France that was already acutely divided in its political allegiances: some conservative French citizens were already prepared to accept alliance with Hitler as preferable to continued experiments with a democracy that had allowed communists, socialists, and Jews to govern when the Popular Front came to power in 1936. Other apolitical but unscrupulous French were ready to exploit whatever material opportunities might come their way in the aftermath of defeat. And a large percentage of the working class in France was caught in the curious dilemma of choosing between its patriotic duty and whatever orders the Communist party would receive from Moscow concerning the proper stance to take toward the Occupation. The invasion rolled over a France that had been, moreover, demoralized by poor planning, by its blindness to the nature of Nazi ideology, and by a general military and bureaucratic ineptitude that, for Camus, is the essence of all bureaucracies. Reflections of these multiple confusions find expression in *The Plague*, especially in the administrative hesitations to recognize the true nature of the scourge that has set upon the city and in the administrative caution in the face of an undeniable catastrophe that threatens the lives of all. To put the discussion in a different light—and to show how the open side of the allegory in *The Plague* allows simultaneous readings of history—the teacher might also invite students to consider that the bureaucratic rationalization at work in the novel could apply to Russia's state apparatus as when, during the thirties, Soviet functionaries organized political machinery that would ensure their own execution.

With these references to modern history as a starting point, the teacher can orient the students toward understanding the way in which *The Plague* is a metahistorical work reflecting on the meaning of history and of human experience as described by history. In this perspective it is no accident that the unnamed narrator of the novel presents himself at the outset as a historian or a chronicler of events or that Tarrou's notebooks are also described as the work of a chronicler. These "historians" wish to write a history that is a record of human resistance to evil and oppression. This use of history stands opposed to the use of history that seeks to justify evil and oppression and especially the acceptance of defeat because that defeat is inscribed in history. In fact, after the defeat in 1940 more than a few collaborators called upon future history to justify their ignominious acts, for they saw themselves as accepting a necessary defeat that future history texts would justify as a product of the inevitable course of events. This future history would have been, one supposes, the future chronicles of Nazis looking back on the New Europe they had created. Opposed to this future history that can be written to justify anything retrospectively is *The Plague*'s imaginary version of present history. This history written in the present and documenting an ongoing struggle against the inevitable, against defeat, pestilence, and death—in short, against the absurd—is the only kind that can justify a people's resistance. It is not unlike the history that might be written by a Russian dissident today or, closer to home, a civil rights worker in the American South yesterday.

The Plague refuses grandiose speculation about evil. Rather it shows that the eruption of the absurd into ongoing history disrupted the patterns of daily life in innumerable ways, some grotesque, some comic. Camus's irony is somewhat caustic in this portrayal, for he has the narrator note that his compatriots' humanism had not prepared them for dealing, in terms of daily needs, with a scourge that goes beyond all human measure (and by choosing the inhuman plague as the image of the absurd, Camus emphasizes the very lack of human measure to this evil). The first result of such an inconceivable disruption of life is that human beings are cut off from one another, isolated behind the walls of prison, of the city, of the armed camps that besiege the land. Camus's choice of the city to portray isolation in *The Plague* is most directly motivated by the historical reality of France during the Occupation: after defeating France the German army first partially, then totally occupied the country, leaving the French with no direct means of communication with the civilized world. Existentially, then, most of the French experienced the Occupation as a period of imprisonment during which one might disappear from one day to the next, arrested by the Gestapo or deported to work as slave labor in Hitler's Reich. (Camus was initially afraid that his name was on one of the deportation lists; the bacillus could strike at any moment with instant results.)

Yet, even as men and women are carried away in the night, life must continue with its daily necessities. *The Plague* is perhaps most clearly referential in the way it documents the details of how daily life goes on in the face of an occupying army. The rationing of food, the hedonistic drinking, the reruns of films in the cinemas, the hoarding of scarce goods and the organizing of a black market, the closing of shops left abandoned by the "departed," the imposing of curfews, the creation of "isolation camps" for mass internments, the inordinate demands made on one's physical stamina— these and many other details offer exact parallels with life during the Occupation. It is only with this sense of the reality of daily routine in a land occupied by the absurd that one can make the next imaginative leap that the novel demands: what can be the meaning of resistance in such daily

circumstances in which there seemed to be no hope for the future? For in
the early months of the Occupation virtually no one in occupied France
believed that the Germans would soon, if ever, be defeated.

Resistance to the occupiers developed slowly in France, starting with the
most humble organizing, by very small groups, of ways to disseminate tracts
that might keep some hope alive. This experience stands behind the way
that in *The Plague* Camus draws back from any suggestion that resistance
entails heroics. The history of the Resistance from 1940 until the liberation
in 1944 is as much a history of disappointments and defeats as it is a glorious
chronicle. Camus wishes to show that in times of calamity the oppressed
are obliged to begin slowly their counterattack, with small but constant acts
of resistance that demand great patience as well as courage. Fatigue and
boredom were also enemies opposing resistance; and in the early months of
organizing, Resistance fighters spent countless and what must have seemed
fruitless hours in discussing, waiting, fearful hiding, and expending enormous
effort for tiny and only symbolic gains. As the Resistance struggle slowly
became more militaristic, it also had to take on some of the characteristics
of the Nazi occupier: the willingness to lie, to resort to deceit or any other
tactic to carry on the fight, and finally a willingness to kill the oppressors
and traitors, knowing that innocent victims would later die when the Nazis
sought retaliation.

The Resistance offers, then, a primary lesson in how the need to destroy
the inhuman has a diabolical capacity to convert virtuous persons into the
inhuman themselves—out of virtuous necessity. This motif is found throughout *The Plague*, though perhaps its expression is most fully developed when
Rieux must meditate on Rambert's accusation that Rieux is living "in abstraction." Like the invisible plague bacillus, like the great Nazi machine
that can only be seen in the individual presence of young German soldiers,
evil is an absurd abstraction that kills and, as it kills, obliges resistance to
take on its own abstract forms. Though resistance is a necessity, one must
never forget that mass executions are also undertaken in the name of virtue.
This lesson in ambiguity is the most crucial one that Camus would have us
glean from modern history. And following Camus's lead in *The Rebel*, students should be asked to ponder historical examples ranging from Robespierre and The Terror of 1793 to the Stalinist camps of the thirties; or, more
recently, American bombing in Vietnam and the recent experiments in terror
in Laos (whose French-educated leaders seem to have applied Robespierre
with a Stalinist sense of efficiency).

Resistance must be undertaken with a full awareness that it can transform
itself into an oppressor like the very oppressor that first gave birth to resistance (and the excesses in retaliation that were committed after the liberation in 1944 show that the Resistance movement was hardly exempt from

murderous tendencies). Yet the logic of the absurd requires that one make a choice: either one resists or one accepts the absurd presence of evil. As in occupied France, men and women of goodwill must either accept the inevitable as the only reasonable choice or embrace struggle as an absurd leap of faith—in order to defy the absurd. Initially most of the French reacted in confusion to the Occupation, and many felt, as *The Plague* puts it, that there was no choice but to fall on their knees. In contrast to this acceptance, Tarrou's initiative in creating voluntary sanitary squads represents the kind of modest resistance to the absurd that Camus proposes; whereas Father Paneloux's sermon, urging the citizens of Oran to accept the plague as a blessing, represents the attitude of those who not only accept historical necessity but attempt to convert it into a justification for whatever is.

The contrast between Rieux's work or Tarrou's volunteer activism and Paneloux's sermons illustrates a very real dilemma that the French faced in the Occupation. Many asked themselves if they should begin a hopeless struggle against unprecedented evil or if they should make the best of it, perhaps even finding in this scourge a well-merited punishment, if not some kind of divine retribution for the decadence that many French believed had fallen on France in the twentieth century. Camus's thought on human innocence takes on its full import in the historical context of France's defeat and occupation. For many French were all too willing to see in this defeat a sign of their guilt—guilt for having embraced democratic excesses, for having allowed chaos to reign or political adventurism to have free course, or simply for having strayed from whatever these French took to be the true traditions of the French nation. On both the right and left sides of the political spectrum one finds at the end of the thirties a remarkable consensus about France's decadence. France's defeat could thus be easily interpreted by many as a merited form of punishment for France's faults, for who was finally guilty of these faults, if not the French themselves? The logic of guilt seemed only to demand that one fall before the divine father and beg forgiveness— and Pétain was more than willing to play this role of the castigating father of the nation when he became the leader of the puppet regime established in Vichy. Paneloux's sermons, especially the first one, set forth an analogous kind of thought. This priest, a specialist in Augustine, demands that his followers fall on their knees and repent, recognizing in the plague a merited retribution for their sins. Moreover, in accepting what Paneloux calls the "immutable order" of things, which the reader may take to be God's will or the order of history, the guilty can recognize that evil is really good, for evil leads the guilty back to an understanding that suffering is necessary and hence justified. Echoing in Paneloux's words that justify evil is a kind of masochistic luxuriating in defeat, especially as he describes the angel of the plague to be as beautiful as Lucifer. One hears reverberations of Vichy rhetoric as well as a fascinated admiration of evil, a self-accusatory admiration that many French felt as they watched the blond troops of the conqueror, resplendent in their machine-like order, march unopposed down the Champs Elysées in Paris. Here were angels of Satan that could be taken to be divine messengers, at least by those predisposed to fall down and proclaim their guilt.

Like almost every other element in this open allegory, Paneloux's position points to the political debates that began as the Occupation came to an end and, in those days of uncertain hopes about political reform or revolution, as the French began to debate about the kind of state they wanted to see replace the discredited Third Republic. The emergence of the Communist party as the most powerful political group in the Resistance and the desire for revolutionary change by many noncommunist French meant that a debate about ends and means in politics became a central political issue. It was no idle question, then, when one asked in the months preceding and following the liberation if the communist desire to maximize the eventual happiness of humankind on earth could justify the revolutionary terrorism that the realization of such a goal might demand. Paneloux may be a specialist in Augustine, but his position also recalls the Hegelian theodicy that offers a doctrine saying evil and suffering are necessary in historical terms to produce the final good embodied in the rational state.

Paneloux's sermon would demonstrate that suffering is necessary if divine providence is to be realized. Once divine providence is identified with history, as in Hegel's thought (and, one could argue, in Marx's), then the conditions are ready for what Camus saw as the rational terrorism of the twentieth century: the elimination of all those who oppose the movement of history. Communists believed that the elimination of those guilty of the objective sin of opposing a classless society was justified by the happiness of the greatest number. Intellectuals such as Camus were not so certain that the ultimate goal of a just state could ever justify murder—any more than the miserable death of a child in *The Plague* might be justified by an eternity of bliss in heaven.

In presenting these issues to a class, the teacher must reckon with both the students' previous exposure to anticommunist indoctrination and their ignorance of the philosophical and political justifications of, say, the Stalinist regime that were prevalent among supporters of the European left during the forties and fifties. The debate between, on the one hand, intellectuals like Camus and Koestler and, on the other hand, noncommunist but prorevolutionary intellectuals like Sartre and Merleau-Ponty can provide a good focal point for these questions. Reflections of this debate are found in Camus's analysis of Stalinism and state terror in *The Rebel*. (And, in a sense, these arguments are a sequel to arguments the student must already have grasped in order to read *Man's Fate*.) I would insist, moreover, that it is the teacher's task to make both sides of the question intelligible. Students are already convinced, by and large, that communism is absolute evil. The teacher, then, needs to show that a socialist revolution has a rational and ethical plausibility that explains why many French were and are willing to entertain the notion that the ultimate good realized by a just society can justify the imposition of a dictatorship of the proletariat and the terrorism that may accompany this seizure of power.

These political debates of the forties also find expression in the conversation between Rieux and Tarrou. Tarrou gives direct voice to the political views that Camus expressed in the newspaper *Combat* and in other essays of the time: he refuses any political state that depends on legalized murder for its foundation. This refusal is a rejection of the apocalyptic revolutionary ambitions that, unknown to those who have them, are carriers of the plague. But Rieux's reserve toward Tarrou's desire for a kind of sanctity also expresses a recognition of the difficult political and moral choices that the world can impose. It was necessary to kill Germans and fellow French citizens to liberate France. Rieux's attitude toward Tarrou reflects a resigned acceptance that pacifism or the refusal to take life may well not be in harmony with the absurd realities of the world. And these absurd realities had become considerably more complex after the defeat of Nazi Germany.

The Plague was published in 1947. Communists initiated strikes that year against the government in which they were participating as coalition partners, war had begun in Indo-China and was about to begin in France's North African colonies, the socialists were losing electoral strength to the right and to the left, and a year later the Berlin airlift clearly signaled that a new era of power politics had begun in earnest. This was the context in which Camus's novel immediately acquired new meanings, transforming this "chronicle" about the recent plague years into a moral parable about man's possibility for action in a world of struggle for liberation and social justice, of continuing tyranny and repression, though now a world capable of self-annihilation.

APPENDIX

Suspecting that the Occupation might mean as much to contemporary students as the Peloponnesian War, I recently asked, without prior notice, an advanced French class (that included students who had studied in France) to write a brief definition of the Occupation. The results ranged from satisfactory answers to admissions of total ignorance. Between these responses, approximately equal in number, were such delightful confusions as those saying that the Russians had invaded France or that the Occupation took place in the Middle Ages. Therefore, I do not think that I can insist strongly enough on the necessity of placing a history of France in the student's hands. Students are, moreover, grateful for the possibility of acquiring knowledge that is essential to their reading and general education. For purposes of economy I have usually had them purchase Alfred Cobban's *A History of Modern France*, a Pelican paperback whose third volume in the 1965 revised edition covers the period from 1871 to 1962. An equally inexpensive *(ou presque)* work in French is Jacques Madaule's *Histoire de France* in Gallimard's Collection Idées. Volume 3, *De la IIIe à la Ve République*, offers a spirited Gaullist account of the Occupation. For a more expensive, but more condensed, one-volume account, one could use Gordon Wright, *France in Modern Times*. More advanced students can be referred to the fundamental work of Robert Aron: *Histoire de Vichy*, *Histoire de la libération*, and the three-volume *Histoire de l'épuration*. Specifically on Resistance organization is Henri Michel's *Histoire de la Résistance en France* in the inexpensive series "Que sais-je?" published frequently in new editions by the Presses Universitaires.

Biographical Context and Its Importance to Classroom Study

Martha O'Nan

Thinking about the biographical context of Albert Camus's *The Plague*, I began to wonder whether the arcades I had seen in Oran in the summer of 1981 were those on the street where the author had lived, whether there could be any real people in the novel from Oran, a city where Mme Camus had taught during her years in Oran, and why people in Oran do not appear to like the book. In seeking answers to these questions, I wrote to Emmanuel Roblès, who is now a well-known writer in Paris but who was born and reared in Oran and was one of Camus's long-time acquaintances. On 8 October 1982, Roblès wrote for each question an answer that I have translated:

1. Yes, there were arcades in Oran (they still exist), and they border the large apartment buildings in the center of the city, on the left side of the street formerly named Arzew when you look in the direction of the eastern suburbs. Camus and his young wife lived in one of these apartment buildings, above these arcades, at number 65, if my memory is right, during 1941–42 (spring 1942). Not far away, on the Place des Victoires was a Jewish institute for Jewish students whom Vichy laws had driven out of the public high schools. Camus taught philosophy in this institute, and [Mme Camus] taught mathematics. The program, French Studies, directed by André Benichou, left Camus enough free time for work on *The Plague*. [Benichou had been a high school teacher in Oran and was forbidden by Vichy to teach in a public school because he was Jewish.]

I add that during that period, I lived near Tlemcen with my wife. Camus had sent me a French Resistance fighter who had to flee from France and whom I had to slip clandestinely to the Moroccan border and hand over to a priest from Lalla Marnia, a town on the other side of the border. . . . In my *Hauteurs de la ville*, I use this little adventure and relate how in the forest we stumbled on a typhus camp, guarded by Senegalese soldiers. That camp had numerous tents where families were forbidden to go. I talked about that to Camus, who was very interested in various details. Soon afterward, my wife herself came down with typhus. That was another story for Camus when I went from Tlemcen to Oran. (My mother lived on Brancia Street very near Arzew, and, when I went to see her, I took the opportunity to visit Camus and his wife.) There were numerous deaths from typhus because the Pasteur Institute in Algiers didn't have vaccines. I myself, under orders from my doctor to be vaccinated, had to wait, by the side of my sick wife, until the vaccines arrived from the Pasteur Institute in Toulouse [in southern France].

Camus used the fact about prohibiting people from moving around freely in areas where there was an epidemic so that it might not be spread.

2. No, there are no people from Oran in *The Plague*. Everything is imagined, as far as characters are concerned.

3. Mme Camus (Francine Faure) before her marriage gave mathematics lessons to my brother (or half brother) Gilbert, today a high school teacher. . . . Therefore, I knew Miss Faure. . . .

4. The people of Oran don't like *The Plague* very much because, in their opinion, the beginning is not very flattering to their city. Camus showed me (when we were in Paris) some anonymous letters from Oran that criticized him at great length. But their anger came not because there were no Arabs in the work but because the city of Oran in the book is a mythical city without any true resemblance to the real Oran, which has not had ramparts since the beginning of the century, ramparts that, it is true, Camus refers to just by suggesting them. See the beginning of part 2 [of *The Plague*]: "But once the town gates were shut. . . ." Perhaps Camus was thinking of the great plague (as deadly as an earlier one in Venice) that had ravaged the city in the eighteenth century. There still exists a cemetery near Raz-el Aïn, just below the city, designated by the French as a historical monument, where there are tombs of victims of the plague and cholera—the plague was followed in the beginning of the nineteenth century by a cholera epidemic that was just as dreadful as the plague had been.

Among his observations, Roblès includes a very significant point: Oran in *The Plague* is a mythical city. The mythical quality is emphasized by Camus in a letter to Roland Barthes: "many of your remarks are clarified by the simple fact that I do not believe in realism in art . . ." (*Essays* 340).

Typical of the reaction from those expecting a real city is the following passage from an article assailing Camus a few months after the appearance of *The Plague* in 1947:

> I am homesick for Oran, in spite of *The Plague*, in spite of all those, including Albert Camus, who have a very bad opinion of this city. "No birds," they say, "no trees and no love." Ha!
>
> No birds in Oran? But where did all those birds come from that woke me up every morning . . . ?
>
> How could the Oranais not be aware of beauty, intelligence, love,

when they have the most beautiful sunset on the Mediterranean? The sunset is seen best of all when a man has one of the most sculptural, beautiful women anywhere in the world by his side and looks in the direction of the waters of Mers-el-Kébir.   (Rousselot 13, 15)[1]

But Camus never had nostalgic memories of Oran as an exotic seaside resort on the Mediterranean. He always felt the presence of unforeseen, inexplicable powers that he expressed as an apprehension. In 1936–37, while directing a theater group on tour in Algerian towns and villages, he wrote: "In the morning, the tenderness and fragility of the Oranais region, so hard and violent under the daytime sun. . . . Everything heralds a glorious day. But with a delicacy and gentleness that one feels will soon be over" (*Notebooks* 31).

The severity of the beauty at Oran was also observed by Camus's favorite teacher, Jean Grenier, who published in 1937 an essay about the glorious light on the pine-covered mountain topped by the old Spanish fort Santa Cruz: the light there, he wrote, "speaks to the intelligence," and one can look down at "the city and the sea and the lake and the mountain at Tlemcen. That pile of white coins stacked haphazardly was Oran; that violet ink splotch was the Mediterranean; that golden dust on a silver mirror was the salt of the plain caught in the sun" (17–18).

In 1937 Camus was twenty-four years old, "thin and pale. . . . He had been seriously ill since adolescence. . . . [He] was very poor then and lived by tutoring students in philosophy and by odd jobs. . . . [He] directed a young theater group . . . , was busy at the Maison de la Culture and . . . soon was to be editor of the *Alger-républicain*" (Depierris 43–48). The Maison de la Culture was encouraged by the Algerian Communist party, which Camus had joined in 1934 but left because of the party's anticolonial policy in Algeria. In the Chamber of Deputies in Paris the Communists opposed the 1936 Blum-Violette Bill, which would have given French citizenship and the right to vote to a few educated Algerian Moslems. A petition supporting the Blum-Violette Bill was circulated under the auspices of the Maison de la Culture, but the real defeat of the bill came from the tooth-and-nail resistance of the large landowners in Algeria, the *colons* who said that they would "never tolerate the possibility that even in the smallest commune an Arab might be a mayor" (Gordon 41).

Camus came into direct contact with the power of the *colons* when he went in 1939 to the Department of Oran to gather information on the case of Michel Hodent for the newspaper the *Alger-républicain*. In a series of thirteen articles, Camus lined up the two sides of the case: the accused, the innocent Hodent, who had followed exactly the Government Office of Wheat rules for buying wheat; and the accusers, an "elite of *colons*, Caïds [powerful native administrators], and Government administrators" who had decided to prevent Hodent from doing his job and diminishing their profits (*Fragments d'un combat* 395).

These articles about the misuse of court power in the Department of Oran were followed by many newspaper reports equally irritating to the governor general of Algeria. Among the painful headlines appearing in the *Alger-républicain* were:

> Speaking in Sarrebruck Hilter Congratulates Himself for the Annexation of Austria and the Sudetes. Vituperates the Jews and Tells the English to Go to Hell

> Japan, Italy, and the Reich Conclude a Military Alliance

> *Alger-républicain* and *Oran-républicain*, Victims of the Censorship of Mr. Daladier

While on the Hodent case in Tiaret and Trézel, both towns in the Department of Oran, Camus went to Oran to see Francine Faure, whom he wanted to marry. She had just interrupted her study of mathematics in France and had returned home to teach. Alluding to her old Oran family, she pointed out that her Berber-Jewish blood made her belong to the oldest inhabitants of Algeria (Lottman, *Camus* 183).

During those visits to Oran, Camus wrote "The Minotaur, or Stopping in Oran" (*Essays* 109–33), a work dedicated to Pierre Galindo, who helped him make plans to marry and who was to facilitate the landing of American troops in Oran in November 1942 (Lottman, *Camus* 185). Camus's Minotaur is a metamorphosis of the animal described in James George Frazer's *Golden Bough*, which Camus had read. Even more changed than the Minotaur is Oran, which is not the growing city, celebrated in the centenary of France in Algeria (1830–1930). Camus sees only ugly buildings, dusty streets that turn into muddy mires, culture exhibited in boxing, an abundance of undertakers, shop windows full of all the bad taste of Europe and the Orient, and the house of the *colon*, with its master wearing a bow tie and white sun helmet to receive "the homage of a procession of slaves clad as nature intended" ("Minotaur" 124).

Possibly the Minotaur has been "sold" on Oran by the exaggerated advertisements that Camus says go to "American extremes" to sell the public on third-rate attractions, announced as "magnificent," "splendid," "extraordinary," "marvellous," "overwhelming," and "stupendous" (113). But the Minotaur appears to be so bored in Oran that he just stops and quickly puts out to sea. Perhaps the bull-bodied, man-headed monster finds his possible victims too dull: the maidens, all "Marlenes" because they imitate the movie actress, and the "guys," all "Clarques" who are fashionably dressed like gangsters (114–15).

Ignoring the pride of the French in their Oran, Camus launched such a critical and humorous attack on the city that he quite likely irritated the censors, who refused permission for the essay to be published in 1939. The spirit of the 1930s in Oran is found in the guidebook published under the patronage of the "high personnage" of the prefect of Oran:

> The city and the port have had an unbelievable growth. From 1832 to the present day the population has increased from 4,300 inhabitants to 265,000. . . . One of the principal ports on the Mediterranean, there was in 1929, the prodigious figure of 11,590 ships with 21 million tonnage. . . . Everywhere, there are splendid stores, huge banks, administrative and commercial buildings. . . . France . . . has made Oran one of the most beautiful cities of France and one of the greatest ports on the Mediterranean where it is good to live. Oran looks toward the future. (*Guide* 220–21)

Listed in this guidebook are 15 dance schools, 31 movie houses, sports covering four pages, 24 banks, 78 dentists, and 356 physicians.

Stemming from the centenary is the scholarly *Oran: Etude de géographie et d'histoire urbaine*, written by René Lespès and published in 1938. In the extensive information about the region, Lespès shows a discreet pride in Oran, especially in its huge, magnificent deep port at Mers-el-Kébir, which he stated was becoming the "Gibraltar of Algeria" (14). Certainly this book must have been sold in Oran bookstores and circulated among local intellectuals such as Francine Faure and her suitor Albert Camus. It describes a walled Oran, a Spanish Oran of 1732, an Oran perfect for Camus's *The Plague*. Equally important for readers who want to know where the characters go on their worrisome business is a city map of the late 1930s.

During the period of 1938–43, when Camus was writing both "Le Minotaur" and *The Plague*, Oran was full of construction in the port area (the Cayla Project) and elsewhere. Extensive construction work was under way: the old Spanish Fort Sainte Thérèse was being torn down to make way for a railroad tunnel underneath, the ramparts on the south side of the city were being demolished to allow for expansion, and Oran in general was being "embellished." The work is described by Camus:

> Clinging to immense slopes are rails, pick-up trucks, cranes, and miniature railroads. . . . Through whistles, dust, and smoke, toylike locomotives twist around vast blocks of stone under a devouring sun. Night and day a nation of ants swarms over the smoking carcass of the

mountain. . . . At regular intervals, in the dead of the night or in the middle of the day, explosions shake the whole mountain and raise the very sea itself. ("Minotaur" 126–27)

The purpose of all the work in Oran is wealth, writes Camus in *The Plague*: "Our citizens work hard, but solely with the object of getting rich. Their chief interest is in commerce, and their chief aim in life is, as they call it, 'doing business' " (Knopf 4).

Not far from the Rue d'Arzew, where Camus visited Francine and where they lived for eighteen months after their marriage in France on 3 December 1940, is the cathedral, a lavish neo-Byzantine church with white towers and facade mosaics on a gold background, opened in 1913 and consecrated in 1930. This is where Father Paneloux preaches two sermons in *The Plague*.

Being a member of the Oran Geographical Society and having an interest in ancient inscriptions, Father Paneloux certainly knows about the history of the old cathedral in Oran, built by the Spanish in 1679, destroyed by an earthquake in 1790, restored in 1831–39, and used as the cathedral until 1930. The old cathedral, between the Casbah and the port, is near the Porte d'Espagne, associated with the visit of Cardinal Ximénez de Cisneros in 1509 to celebrate the successful end of the "crusade" of the Spanish in Oran. Also nearby is the Place de la Perle, crossed by Cervantes in 1581. Cervantes wrote an exciting play, *El gallardo español*, set in Oran and presented there four centuries later in the adaptation by Emmanuel Roblès. Two other plays by Cervantes, *El trato de Argel* and *Los baños de Argel*, are set in Algiers, the latter being published by Camus in his *Rivages* in the translation by Jeanne Sicard.

Another great interest of Father Paneloux is Augustine, for whom Camus had special enthusiasm. Augustine spent most of his life just a few miles from Mondovi (now Dréan), the village near Bône (now Annaba), where Camus was born. In his letters about Roman North Africa, Augustine (354–430) speaks of many problems—ironically almost the same as those found by Camus during his lifetime: the cultivation of large estates by exploited natives; the shipments of wheat, wine, and olives across the Mediterrean; and the imposition of foreign institutions, laws, and language.[2] The social concerns of Augustine appear to be "between the lines" of the sermons as reported by Dr. Rieux.

In the beginning of *The Plague*, Dr. Rieux has just seen his wife off at the station—no doubt, the beautiful mosque-style station still in use in the southern part of the city. The physician most likely sends his patients to the hospital completed in 1936, the Hôpital Civil composed of some thirty separate buildings with a total of 520 beds. A new feature of the hospital was the ambulance service that Dr. Rieux uses several times for his patients. In the center of town, he often walks under the palm and fig trees of the Place d'Armes, bordered on one side by the Municipal Office with its famous lions by Cain and dominated on the other side by the gilt domes of the opera, where two characters attend Gluck's *Orpheus.* Even in the Place d'Armes rats begin to appear and are perhaps outward and visible signs of France's corrupt city government housed nearby.

A few blocks away from the Municipal Office is the prefect at the prefecture. The prefect, however, appears to be a man who is rarely approached directly and who may represent the lack of understanding that France was showing in Algeria—a lack so clearly expressed by Camus's friend Jules Roy, who tried to tell the story of Algeria to a "chloroformed France" (*War* 13). The journalist Raymond Rambert in *The Plague* has traveled to Oran with the same intention, although Dr. Rieux doubts that Rambert will be allowed to tell the truth about the Arabs in a Paris newspaper.

But Oran is an ironic place to come to investigate the Arab story. There, during the 1930s, the Arabs were isolated in the Village nègre; they represented 23.7% of the population but had neither citizenship nor voting rights. The dominant European population represented 74% in "the most 'European' city of Algeria," a statement issued with pride and displayed in bold print in *Oran: Etude de géographie et d'histoire urbaine* by Lespès. By 1962, the year the Algerian revolution ended, there were some 300,000 Europeans in Oran, most of whom had to be repatriated.

Unlike those miserable and unwilling repatriates (*pieds-noirs*), many characters in *The Plague* have only one pleasant place in mind: Paris. Grand, "a humble employee in local administration," suffers twenty-two years "studiously revising the tariff of the town baths or gathering for a junior secretary the materials of a report on the new garbage-collection tax" (41). He finds escape in the single sentence that he constantly revises: "One fine morning in the month of May an elegant young horsewoman might have been seen riding a handsome sorrel mare along the flowery avenues of the Bois de Boulogne" (96). Even the critic of France, Rambert, whiles away the tedium in thinking about "unsummoned vistas of old stones and riverbanks . . . and many another scene of [Paris] he'd never known he loved so much, and these mental pictures [kill] all desire for any form of action" (101).

These two characters never suspect that their hidden, visionary ambition to reach Paris through Oran shows them to be "strangers" not only in Algeria but in France and the world. Even history cannot teach them. Grand, for example, slavishly learns Latin because he has been "told that a knowledge of Latin gives one a better understanding of the real meanings of French words" (30). But he remains culturally blind, never even approaching Camus's conclusions on the sad contributions that the Romans made in Algeria. Camus visited the extensive ruins left by the Romans at Djémila in Eastern

Algeria and at Tipasa between Oran and Algiers, places where he found "something forged that gives man the measure of his identity" and where the Romans, like the Europeans in Oran, "marked [Africa] with their non-commissioned officer's civilization. They had a vulgar and ridiculous idea of greatness, measuring the grandeur of their empire by the surface it covered" (*Essays* 74, 79).

Much of Oran, like the Roman civilization, was to be destroyed as Camus knew. First, the British sank part of the French fleet in Mers-el-Kébir on 3 July 1940 to keep the fleet from serving Nazi Germany. Then, Operation Torch began on 8 November 1942, with Allied invasions of Casablanca, Algiers, and Oran. In 1943 President Roosevelt arrived on the *Iowa* at Mers-el-Kébir, the only Mediterranean port large enough to accommodate such a huge ship. In August 1944 Mers-el-Kébir served as a base for the Allied invasion of Europe.

The dramatic, tragic situation of Oran in the 1940s is not realistically presented in *The Plague*, a novelistic chronicle that fuses many of Camus's observations into an "epidemic." He found the germs of the "epidemic" reappearing in the ageless attempts of peoples from Europe and Asia to remain permanently on the shores of what is now Algeria: the Phoenicians, the Romans, the Turks, the Spanish, and the French. The health of these momentous undertakings was always undermined by some "illness" originating from human beings, politics, or the gods—a "plague" that Albert Camus suggests can come suddenly to throw humankind into an impossible struggle.

NOTES

[1] All translations from French are mine except when a translator is listed.

[2] Students might enjoy reading Augustine, *Select Letters*, trans. James Houston Baxter (Cambridge: Harvard Univ. Press, 1930).

The North African Context of *The Plague*

Catharine Savage Brosman

My purpose in this essay is at once to indicate how one can assess and convey to students the role of the North African context in *The Plague* and to furnish a model (among many) for the teaching of background in other works of fiction. While well aware that no one element—particularly setting—can by itself create a novel of lasting significance and that *The Plague*'s setting has a more limited function than in certain other works by Camus, I believe that the identification and analysis of its role can be not only an interesting experience in itself but also a valuable lesson in the reading of fiction. The study of settings helps the unsophisticated student learn that a novel is more than plot and that meaning comes from a variety of aspects and their inter-relations—a lesson applicable to other genres as well. In other words, students can be taught to thematize by using settings. This approach is, moreover, practical: though our aims as literature teachers are not narrow, we must often in our rapid treatment show our students how to achieve an idea of the whole from a few vantage points only. The less obtrusive the aspect, the more it needs to be examined and its place in the fictional fabric clarified. The complex symbolism of *The Plague* and its tendency toward abstractions can keep the student from seeing that in this novel—as in *The Stranger* and other pertinent Camusian works, such as "The Adulterous Woman"—the context is not merely an unimportant reflection of the author's Algerian roots: for him, as for many other modern writers, landscape and cityscape are cor-relatives of emotions, states of mind, mental adventures, and metaphysical questionings, while not usually serving simply as one-dimensional symbols.

Whether the work is read in French or in English, in an advanced course on the novel or in an introductory course to modern literature, the instructor ordinarily needs to give some information about Camus as a North African writer, especially when little outside reading is required. It is useful, for instance, to point out that, though he is the best known, Camus is not the only noteworthy recent French author who comes from Algeria. Indeed, an important group of poets, critics, and novelists called the School of Algiers and associated with the publishing house of Edmond Charlot flourished before World War II in North Africa, moving to Paris after the war. One can mention the names of Emmanuel Roblès (who told Camus about the typhus outbreak near Oran in 1941), Max-Pol Fouchet, Jules Roy, Gabriel Audisio, and Jean Amrouche, most of whom were friends of Camus, at least at one time. This group is not to be considered as representative of an indigenous literary movement; with the exception of Amrouche, all these authors were of European descent. But they differed from their counterparts in Europe, and in some ways they laid the groundwork for a later Arab-Berber literature written in French. Their writings are frequently concerned with Algeria's landscape, history, people, and peculiar situation as united to France until 1962 and yet separate and so different from the mother country that it produced its own cultural traditions. These writers were characteristically sensitive to the North African scenery and light, particularly after they had settled elsewhere: as *The Plague* shows, alienation heightens consciousness.

But they were not just regionalists, if one understands by that writers dedicated chiefly to depicting the character and mores of a geographical and culturally distinct area. Moreover, they were not initially concerned primarily with the colonial question, although some, such as Roy, eventually wrote in favor of independence and most were generally sympathetic toward their Muslim compatriots. Camus is still widely blamed in the liberal press on both sides of the Atlantic for not having taken the side of the Arab nationalists during the Algerian conflict. Conor Cruise O'Brien has suggested that *The Plague*, like *The Stranger*, reveals Camus's colonialist conditioning (Lazere, "American Criticism" 409). Despite the dominant Mediterranean setting, his fiction tends toward the metaphysical and is ultimately concerned with the situation of modern humanity as a whole. Although, according to Amiel's famous phrase, "a landscape is a state of the soul," Camus in *The Plague* is less interested in personal emotion projected onto nature than in the reflection of a general human situation. It has been observed that space in this novel seems generalized, almost mythologized (Lévi-Valensi, in Gay-Crosier, *Camus, 1980* 62–63). In this connection the instructor can point out that one of the challenges of all fiction that aspires to be more than a story is to indicate generality through particularity.

Setting is a compositional element in most mimetic fiction, giving a mental image against which the action may be followed and characters delineated, contributing to a work's persuasiveness and its mental reality for us, and thus helping to convey themes. But it can also be both directly and symbolically expressive. The topic of *The Plague* needed a setting that could easily lend itself to symbols and abstractions, while remaining basically realistic (since Camus was writing neither a fable nor a genuine allegory). Oran and its desert surroundings, to which his imagination readily gravitated, seem well suited. All literature, especially symbolic, thrives on extremes and oppositions; the desert offers such extremes. Since it also affords a certain aesthetic distance, it is more suitable than a locale in occupied France would have been, even though the latter would have fit one of the most generally recognized interpretations of the text. The desert has long represented a place of contemplation and moral testing. Furthermore, the consolations of nature are fewer there than in more temperate climates. The penchant toward such harsh landscapes in a writer known for his moderation may seem surprising. But it was on the practical and political planes that Camus was moderate; metaphysically and stylistically (even personally sometimes), he was inclined toward excesses and antitheses. Moreover, any North African city can be considered more isolated than European ones, since the surroundings are generally sparsely inhabited; in addition, North Africa is less historical than Europe, at least to the Western reader, and more pagan (and this underscores the dubious applicability of Paneloux's arguments).

These observations can help students understand the role of the desert background. The urban setting deserves a few additional comments. Accounts of plagues are often largely centered on cities and their surroundings; such are Defoe's *A Journal of the Plague Year*, Pepys's eyewitness account of the Great Plague of London, and, among modern French writers, Jean Giono's narrative in *The Horseman on the Roof* of a cholera epidemic in southern France. Physically favorable to the spread of disease, the confined urban settings emphasize on the literary plane the force of the scourge and the helplessness of its victims. Biographical and geographic factors help explain the choice of Oran over other Algerian cities. Though published after World War II, the novel was planned and partly written during the war, and it reflects something of the author's situation then. He had been familiar with Oran previously but became better acquainted with it in 1941 (when the action of the novel is supposed to take place, according to the manuscript), when he returned from France with his bride, Francine, to live there with her and her mother. He was ill: his tuberculosis had flared up seriously. In August 1942, leaving for what he thought would be a short stay, he went to a mountainous area near St.-Etienne, France, in the expectation that this change of climate would be favorable. The Allied landings in November, which put an end to virtually all communication with French territories in North Africa, extended the separation beyond what he had anticipated. Thus, in a reverse situation from that of Rieux in the novel, it was the husband who was ill, separated by the absurd chances of war from his wife in Oran and suffering from what seemed like exile—which students will recognize as one of his most persistent literary obsessions.

After this classroom excursion onto biographical territory, which, certain critical objections notwithstanding, is valid as well as interesting for undergraduates, the instructor can note the topographical peculiarities of Oran (second in size among Algerian cities and a major port, but more isolated than Algiers). Built on cliffs that rise from a bay and that are quite majestic when viewed from sea or air, the tiered city does not have the easy approach to beach and port that makes many other seaside towns appealing; as Camus says, it turns its back on the sea and is thus "closed" even before sanitary measures seal it off. It does not offer readily what he calls elsewhere "nuptials" between a human being and nature. He exaggerates its separation from the water, however; in truth, the Mediterranean is visible from a number of locations in the city. He also distorts its appearance, stressing its lack of trees and general unattractiveness (in fact, there are fine palms and other species, some of which he mentions himself); it could almost be the gloomy St.-Etienne of occupied France. From the very first pages, where the narrator begins his chronicle by describing Oran, the city seems a geographic correlative of the pessimistic note struck by the title. Yet for Camus Algeria always represented happiness, a place of beauty and passion. Oran, then, is its own contradiction; it is almost Manichean.

This *is*, however, a Mediterranean world, and the rest of my essay focuses on the characteristically North African elements (sun, sky, sea, desert, and mountains), their contrasts and tensions, and their symbolic value. Numerous commentaries on sun and water symbolism in Camus have been published (e.g., by S. B. John and R. Quilliot [in Brée, *Essays* 132–44 and 38–47] and by E. Roblès), but few of them analyze the use of these elements in *The Plague*. I offer the following remarks as a guide to class commentary. First, one needs to note that elements such as sun, wind, and sea are, after the initial description, repeatedly mentioned, particularly at crucial moments such as the janitor's death, Paneloux's sermons, the death of the judge's son, the arrival of the news of Mme Rieux's death, and, of course, the swimming scene and its prelude on the terrace. At the conclusion, it is while Rieux is meditating on Oran from the terrace that he decides to compose his chronicle. Second, it can be observed that the Mediterranean climate and landscape have a dual value, positive and negative, that is part of the system of oppositions in the book. Their beauty is often visible, always implied; but the more beautiful the landscape appears, the greater the antithesis with the human suffering brought about by the plague. Death always seems more absurd when contrasted with beauty (hence the traditional association between death and a lovely woman). And it would appear that other evils, too, are worse when contrasted with a scene of great natural appeal.

Here the ambiguity of the plague symbolism must be discussed. If the plague stands only for itself (a disease), then it is a *natural* evil, and nature should be viewed as potentially hostile; the disease is a striking extension of the harshness already visible in the Algerian landscape. If the plague stands for *moral* evil (the war, the Occupation, and all other inhumanity of man to man), then nature, furnishing merely the symbol, can in contrast be seen as much more benign. In that case, it is the quiet beauty of the panorama stretching beyond Oran to the hills, the purity of the sky at night, the fraternal warmth of the water that should be stressed. Insofar as the plague represents *metaphysical* evil, then nature, which is its locus, can never be truly friendly to humanity; the divorce that *The Myth of Sisyphus* identifies as the absurd is built into their copresence. In any case, one notes the incommensurability between nature and the human situation.

This ambiguity of nature in Camus's work is never resolved, as an examination of the background elements reveals. The sun is both friendly and murderous (in *The Stranger*, almost a malevolent force and in *The Plague*, an oppressive presence and a contributing factor to the spread of pestilence); it is associated with death and irrationality. The Algerian blue sky, so visible in this treeless site—dazzling in the daytime, softened at twilight—is the single visual escape for the imprisoned citizens, giving an outlet to their aspirations and longings for a fraternal world. Sometimes it blends with the sea and palpitates as if alive. But at night, scintillating, it is again as hard as quartz. Yet, whatever the sky's connotations, Camusian heroes seem to need it to come to terms with themselves. The wind is often hot, burning and feverish, or dusty, and it can carry contagion, thus acting as the enemy of happiness. Yet it can be humanized, bringing sounds and smells of ordinary activity in Oran; it can cleanse and liberate, sweeping the sky of gloomy mists and clouds, carrying away human sounds, revealing the stars, and bringing freshness from the sea. In the episode of Tarrou's confession, the rising wind, carrying a sea smell, and the sound of waves may be interpreted as an invitation to life and action, like that at the end of Paul Valéry's "The Cemetery by the Sea." The sea, which has strong emotional overtones in Camus's works generally, is the friendliest of the natural elements. It is evoked repeatedly in connection with the desire to escape, and, in the crucial swimming scene, it offers a ritual cleansing that seals the friendship of Rieux and Tarrou and washes away, as it were, the contagion of disease; it is free like an animal, vital, sensual, and fraternal. (The instructor can point out that Camus, an enthusiastic swimmer, had himself spent many hours on the beaches in Algiers and persisted in going bathing at Oran although his wife told him it was bad for his tuberculosis. The sense of union with a cosmic element seemed to suit his metaphysical drive.) Yet even in this scene, a cold current reminds us that the sea is indifferent; moreover, like the desert, it is sterile. Elsewhere Camus makes the water stand for what is restless and troublesome in the world, that is, human nature itself. These four elements—sun, sky, wind, sea—are all connected thematically to death.

At this point it would be suitable to recall again the definition of the absurd in *The Myth of Sisyphus* and show that—despite the common view that holds that in *The Plague* Camus was more human, more positive, and more reconciled to life than in his previous works—this novel still has much in common with them. This commonality is revealed partly by the setting. For even if nature is not tragic, the presence of human beings in it remains so. The desert—as the lives of the saints show—is not a refuge from destiny but rather a place to confront it, and, without faith and with lucidity, destiny is tragic. The repeated Camusian insistence on awareness—knowing oneself and one's position, facing irrationality with reason—is supported here by the whole complex of desert imagery: the sun (despite its negative connotations) bringing light and perspective, perhaps symbolizing the unity of rationality; the uninterrupted view toward what Camus calls the "luminous hills," which puts no obstacle or distraction between human beings and their thoughts; the way the landscape feeds human aspirations toward liberation, grandeur, elevation, and oneness with nature, which are inevitably qualified by a smallness of stature; the barren stretches conveying the nothingness of civilization and human individuality, the certainty of mortality. In this wasteland Oran is an island (Camus has a fondness for island imagery), an image of universal striving toward love and fulfillment, but an ironically unhappy one; what S. B. John has called Oran's "mineral landscape" (qtd. in Brée, *Camus: A Collection* 136) shows how much the city partakes of the surrounding desert, which will ultimately reclaim Oran and the human life it reveals. Even at the conclusion of the story, Rieux's view over the sea and hills puts into perspective the joyous celebration marking the plague's end and reminds him of nature's indifference. As Camus said in *The Stranger*, there is no way out, no reconciliation between humankind and its destiny.

Less important than the historical and social background and the precise physical characteristics of Oran, then, is a sense of climate, in which the setting conveys at once an acknowledgment of estrangement from the world and a sense of harmony with it, in a typically Camusian contrast. The author deliberately abstracts from the concrete background a feeling of the eternal position of humanity in the universe and, without resorting to the pathetic fallacy, excels in making nature objectify human desires and failures alike. This use of setting, which distinguishes him both from social novelists and specialists in local color, illustrates his contention that fiction should reconcile the singular and the universal. When Rieux concludes that our true homeland is found burnt on the walls of the city, in the fragrant brush of the hills, in the sea, Camus also seems to advise us to love what, in *Nuptials*, he calls "the song of the world" (*Essays* 67) and yet to recognize its indifference. His final counsels must be read in this light.

CODA

On Not Being a Stranger

Mary Ann Caws

"But," said Rambert, "I am a stranger to this city."

The Plague

Reading Camus for the first time is not so different from discovering the self. Between the world of cliché morality and of nuanced, or sophisticated, philosophical problems—addressing them both and serving to bridge them—stands the work of Camus. His personality helps us make the passage from one to the other, in both directions, as the resonance of his language helps us make the passage between literature and the problems of our time.

Speaking for a secular religion of the absurd, if I may put it like that, and provoking our many and various responses to it, Camus's *The Stranger* becomes our own familiar stranger within and without us. Speaking about individual guilt and its haunting interior setting, the double scene of Amsterdam and Paris in *The Fall* makes the backdrop for our own sense of whatever fall from whatever secular grace we may privilege as nearest to us and our individual destiny. Camus's *Caligula* presents evil unadulterated; his "Return to Tipasa" presents a landscape at its most lyric. Sisyphus—as Camus has us climb with him and roll his rock endlessly, uselessly, but not hopelessly—becomes a myth for our time too. Camus represents the Greek heritage in our thought and offers a moral setting for a time needing that tradition.

117

If the fifties seemed simpler, a moment when these fables and tales and problem texts seemed to fit our thoughts, then why in the eighties do we assume we are still addressed by these moral tales? Why does the heroic antihero called Meursault ("the only Christ we deserve," in *The Stranger*) so clearly remain among us? What place can the essential modesty of the universe, so presented, occupy in the rush of our lives, which might often seem inhospitable to such understatement? No eternal statements of a high-blown sort are made here; the myths Camus presents are those "with no other depth than that of human suffering, and, like it, inexhaustible" (*Sisyphus* 87).

We take on finally, says Camus, the face of our own truths: our own visage is formed of what we read, of what problems we linger over, of what half-verities we care about. So the human affection springing up in the strangest of places, between an odd, shuffling man and his mangy dog; or the understanding, under an evening sky, of a mother and her boyfriend at the end of her life; or the essential "metaphysical happiness" of claiming the real absurdity of the world—these phenomena that Camus sets before us have a good chance of becoming our truths, of making us. Don Juan speaks for every person wanting to try out everything, and he is damned only as we are. Meursault, drinking his café au lait and condemned for it, is judged as we are likely to be, on detail. Sisyphus, making his painful way up the mountain with his boulder, only to start over, is not discontented but shares his burden with us: "The struggle itself toward the heights is enough to fill a man's heart. One must imagine Sisyphus happy" (91).

Doomed to making his way, and ours, the absurd hero is not called on to make eternal statements, any more than is the contemporary writer, of the fifties or of our time. As Camus is appropriated, variously, by the Kierke-gaardians, the Schopenhauerians, the Marxists, the "new philosophers" as well as the existential nostalgists, we are called on only to realize that no appropriation is permanent either. "Art and nothing but art," said Nietzsche, "we have art so as not to die from the truth" (qtd. in *Sisyphus* 69).

Defoe, whom Camus cites in the epigraph to *The Plague*, claimed that it was no more unreasonable to represent one kind of imprisonment by another than to represent anything in existence by something not in existence. If, indeed, allegory serves morally and epistemologically as well as didactically, we not only learn about the real by reading about the imagined, but we become involved in the allegorical ethical issues as in the ways of knowing they imply. But no matter what else one can say about them in general, allegories like *The Plague* do not permit our being a stranger to what they stand for, however removed from us or strange they seem, since they represent something we already knew but did not know how to care about.

"Amid the cries ever louder and longer, the multicolored flares of the rockets in the sky . . . Doctor Rieux decided to draw up the account ending like this, so as not to be among the silent ones . . ." (Gallimard 278; trans. mine). Instead, he bears witness "like this," in this text now read, to injustice as to courage and to what endures, in spite of all. Knowing as he does that no definitive victory is to be recounted—when we are honest—and that no city, however happy, can be sure of its lasting health, no joy guaranteed free from menace, he writes of the plague as of the human condition, everywhere and not in one city only. For us, and not only, for example, for the French or Algerian readers of 1947, literature in situation may be the lasting kind.

The book itself bears Camus's witness to the human choice to heal when possible, on both the physical and the mental planes, since the two are intertwined. And, for those to whom it is not given to heal, the choice affirmed is to write of those whose gift it is. There is no option out of humanity and into immunity, nor can health be certified by any mere desire or statement or perception of what seems to be so at the moment. Like "to see" and "to love," "to cure" and "to heal" are temporary verbs and can be cruel ones. Curing now for what future? Any certainty about what follows on "the cure" is not included in the knowledge we bring with us to this city, in appearance doomed. Saving has no lifetime warranty.

For that reason, perhaps, each of the high moments spared from suffering is to be marveled at; a sudden communion of two beings on a lofty terrace above the sea reaches here a summit of emotion and intelligence at once, memorable even in the center of the drama of the book, itself part of history, political science, philosophy, and the literature of the world.

How do we read the themes of terror? From the 1982 book of nuclear fear *When the Wind Blows*, where the homey British couple faces doom, to all doomsday books in general, the sobering effect of what we read, provided we do not eternally distance our reading from our feeling and exile it from whatever place we believe ourselves to occupy, is universal as well as specific. Camus's *The State of Siege*—the play dealing with the plague and the heroism it uncovers, together with the terror—is a state very like our own. The menace of the plague-bearing rats is to be read as near to home; the point where the outer menace of cosmic catastrophe joins the inner ones of unfeeling sensitivity and lack of courage is variable, peculiarly indefinable, and no less urgent to try to define. The effect is infinitely individual, despite the common terror, as are the stress, the sadness, and the loneliness that separate as well as bring together.

We cannot opt endlessly for ignorance. The Socratic choice we used to toy with, as if we could have chosen, between the knowing and the tragic and the unknowing and the cheerful, is no longer ours to make. Although now over the terrace of our minds some outer wind may be blowing with its deadly gift, we will not always necessarily be afflicted from without; the terror is already within, to be awakened. Yet it is here, within, that the great works of literature entertain their dialogue with each of us, not just about plague and what plagues us most deeply but also about joy and what joys we can most deeply share, once we have realized that there are to be no strangers now to any city or to any of the great works concerning all of us: " 'I see,' said Rambert, 'we have to begin everything again' " (148).

PARTICIPANTS IN SURVEY OF CAMUS INSTRUCTORS

The following scholars and teachers of Camus generously agreed to participate in the survey of approaches to teaching *The Plague* that preceded preparation of this volume. Without their invaluable assistance and generous support, the volume simply would not have been possible.

Douglas W. Alden, University of Virginia; Simone Baepler, Valparaiso University; Mark Bernheim, Miami University, Ohio; Marc Bertrand, Stanford University; Konrad Bieber, State University of New York, Stony Brook; Robert R. Brock, University of Montana; Catharine Savage Brosman, Tulane University; Harcourt Brown, Brown University; A. T. J. Cairns, University of Calgary; Mary Ann Caws, Hunter College, City University of New York; Diane G. Crowder, Cornell College; Ronald E. DeBacco, Westmoreland County Community College; Claire L. Dehon, Kansas State University; Pierre E. Demers, Fu Jen University, Taiwan; Alvin Dobsevage, Western Connecticut State University; Cynthia A. Eby, James Madison University; Lois Dahlin Francis, University of California, Berkeley; Ailene S. Goodman, Howard University; David I. Grossvogel, Cornell University; Mary Gutermuth, Sam Houston State University; Pierre Han, American University; Bradley S. Hayden, Western Michigan University; Bette G. Hirsch, Cabrillo College; Eugene Hollahan, Georgia State University; Nancy Jo Hoy, Saddleback College; Sister Irma M. Kashuba, Chestnut Hill College; Katharine A. Knutsen, Sweet Briar College; Richard T. Lambert, Carroll College; Kevin Lewis, University of South Carolina; William J. Maroldo, Texas Lutheran College; Gabriel Moyal, McMaster University; Sister Mary Henry Nachtsheim, College of St. Catherine; Martha O'Nan, State University of New York, Brockport; Anna Otten, Antioch College; David B. Parsell, Furman University; Françoise Ravaux, University of Richmond; Robert F. Roeming, University of Wisconsin, Milwaukee; Bianca Rosenthal, California Polytechnic State University; Mary Jane Schenck, University of Tampa; Jeanne J. Smoot, North Carolina State University; Amie Godman Tannenbaum, Gettysburg College; Susan Tarrow, Cornell University; Allen Thiher,

University of Missouri, Columbia; Eva Van Ginneken, California State University, Fullerton; Paul Von Blum, University of California, Los Angeles; Marianne Cramer Vos, Alabama State University; Jennifer Waelti-Walters, University of Victoria; Louise R. Witherell, University of Wisconsin, Green Bay; Donald I. Yeats, Western Australian Institute of Technology; Richard Ziegfeld, University of South Carolina, Columbia; Eugenia N. Zimmerman, Carleton University.

WORKS CITED

Books and Articles

Alleg, Henri. *La Guerre d'Algérie*. 3 vols. Paris: Temps Actuels, 1982.

Aron, Robert. *Histoire de la libération*. Paris: Fayard, 1959.

———. *Histoire de l'épuration*. 3 vols. Paris: Fayard, 1967–75.

———. *Histoire de Vichy*. Paris: Fayard, 1954.

Auerbach, Erich. *Mimesis: The Representation of Reality in Western Literature*. Trans. Willard R. Trask. 1953. Princeton: Princeton Univ. Press, 1974.

Babbie, Earl. *Science and Morality in Medicine*. Berkeley: Univ. of California Press, 1970.

Barrett, William. *Irrational Man: A Study in Existential Philosophy*. New York: Doubleday, 1958.

Barthes, Roland. *Critical Essays*. Trans. Richard Howard. Evanston: Northwestern Univ. Press, 1972.

———. *Le Degré zéro de l'écriture*. Paris: Editions de Seuil, 1953.

———. *Essais critiques*. Paris: Editions du Seuil, 1964.

———. *Writing Degree Zero*. Trans. Annette Lavers and Colin Smith. Boston: Beacon, 1970.

Barton, Richard G. *Death and Dying*. New York: Van Nostrand, 1978.

Benda, Julien. *La Trahison des clercs*. Paris: J.-J. Pauvert, 1965.

Bersani, Jacques, et al. *La Littérature en France depuis 1945*. Paris: Bordas, 1970.

Bieber, Konrad. *L'Allemagne vue par les écrivains de la Résistance*. Genève: Droz, 1954.

Booth, Wayne C. *The Rhetoric of Fiction*. 2nd ed. Chicago: Univ. of Chicago Press, 1983.

Bourneuf, Roland, and Réal Ouellet. *L'Univers du roman*. Paris: Presses Universitaires, 1975.

Brée, Germaine. ed. *Camus*. 1959. New Brunswick: Rutgers Univ. Press, 1964.

———. *Camus: A Collection of Critical Essays*. Englewood Cliffs: Prentice, 1962.

———. *Camus and Sartre: Crisis and Commitment*. New York: Delacorte, 1972.

Brochier, Jean-Jacques. *Albert Camus: Philosophe pour classes terminales*. Paris: Balland, 1970.

Campbell, Catherine E. "A Survey of Graduate Reading Lists in French." *French Review* 56 (1983): 588–98.

Camus, Albert. *Albert Camus: The Essential Writings*. Ed. Robert E. Meagher. New York: Harper, 1979.

———. *Fragments d'un combat 1938–40*. Vol. 3 of *Cahiers Albert Camus*. Ed. Jacqueline Lévi-Valensi and André Abbou. Paris: Gallimard, 1978.

———. *Lyrical and Critical Essays*. Ed. Philip Thody. Trans. Ellen Conroy Kennedy. New York: Knopf, 1968.

———. *The Myth of Sisyphus and Other Essays*. Trans. Justin O'Brien. New York: Vintage-Knopf, 1955.

———. *Notebooks: 1935–1942*. Trans. Philip Thody. New York: Knopf, 1963.

———. *Œuvres Complètes*. Vol. 1, *Théâtre, Récit, Nouvelles*. Vol. 2, *Essais*. Ed. Roger Quilliot. Bibliothèque de la Pléiade. Paris: Gallimard, 1962 (vol. 1), 1965 (vol. 2).

———. *La Peste*. Paris: Livre de Poche, 1947; Gallimard, 1947; Folio, 1972.

———. *The Plague*. Trans. Stuart Gilbert. New York: Modern Library–Random, 1948; Vintage-Random, 1972; Modern Library College Edition–Random, 1968; Knopf, 1952. London: Hamilton, 1948.

———. *The Rebel*. Trans. Anthony Bower. 1954; rpt. New York: Vintage-Random, 1956.

———. *Resistance, Rebellion and Death*. New York: Modern Library–Random, 1961.

Cazamian, Louis François. *A History of French Literature*. Oxford: Clarendon, 1967.

Charlton, D. G., ed. *France: A Companion to French Studies*. New York: Methuen, 1979.

Cipolla, Carlo M. *Faith, Reason and the Plague in Seventeenth-Century Tuscany*. Trans. Muriel Kittel. Ithaca: Cornell Univ. Press, 1979.

Cobban, Alfred. *A History of Modern France*. New York: Braziller, 1965.

Costes, Alain. *Albert Camus et la parole manquante: Étude psychanalytique*. Paris: Payot, 1973.

Crawfurd, Raymond. *Plague and Pestilence in Literature and Art*. London: Oxford Univ. Press, 1914.

Crochet, Monique. *Les Mythes dans l'œuvre de Camus*. Paris: Editions Universitaires, 1973.

Cruickshank, John. *Albert Camus and the Literature of Revolt*. 1959. New York: Oxford Univ. Press, 1970.

————, ed. *The Novelist as Philosopher: Studies in French Fiction 1935–1960*. New York: Oxford Univ. Press, 1962.

Culler, Jonathan. *Structuralist Poetics: Structuralism, Linguistics and the Study of Literature*. Ithaca: Cornell Univ. Press, 1975.

Dawidowicz, Lucy S. *The War against the Jews 1933–1945*. New York: Holt, 1975.

Defoe, Daniel. *Robinson Crusoe*. Ed. Michael Shinagel. New York: Norton, 1975.

Depierris, Jean-Louis. *Entretiens avec Emmanuel Roblès*. Paris: Seuil, 1967.

Dörrer, Anton, ed. *Hippolytus Guarinonius . . . zur 300. Wiederkehr seines Todestages*. Innsbruck: Universitätsverlag Wagner, 1954.

Fitch, Brian T., ed. *Camus romancier: La Peste. Albert Camus* 8 (1976).

————. *The Narcissistic Text: A Reading of Camus' Fiction*. Toronto: Univ. of Toronto Press, 1982.

Forster, Leonard, ed. *The Penguin Book of German Verse*. London: Penguin, 1961.

Fortier, Paul. *Une Lecture de Camus*. Paris: Klincksieck, 1977.

Frazer, James George. *The Golden Bough: A Study in Magic and Religion*. 13 vols. New York: St. Martin's, 1911–36.

Gaillard, Pol. *La Peste: Albert Camus*. Paris: Hatier, 1972.

Gallant, Mavis. "What did Sartre Do during the Occupation?" *New York Times Book Review*, 4 Apr. 1982, 26, 27.

Gay-Crosier, Raymond. "L'Anarchisme mesuré de Camus." *Symposium* 24 (1970): 243–53.

————, ed. *Albert Camus, 1980*. Gainesville: Univ. Presses of Florida, 1980.

————. "Albert Camus." In *A Critical Bibliography of French Literature*. Ed. R. A. Brooks. Vol. 6, ed. D. W. Alden. Syracuse: Syracuse Univ. Press, 1980, 1573–1679.

Gilligan, Maureen. *The Language of Allegory*. Ithaca: Cornell Univ. Press, 1979.

Girard, René. *Violence and the Sacred*. 1972. Trans. Patrick Gregory. Baltimore: Johns Hopkins Univ. Press, 1977.

Goodman, Ailene S. *Explorations of a Baroque Motif: The Plague in Selected Seventeenth-Century English and German Literature*. Diss. Univ. of Maryland, 1981.

————. "The Surgical Mask in Literature." *Janus* (Amsterdam) 69 (1982): 69–76.

Gordon, David C. *The Passing of French Algeria*. New York: Oxford Univ. Press, 1966.

Gottfried, Robert S. *The Black Death: Natural and Human Disaster in Medieval Europe*. New York: Free, 1983.

Greene, Robert W. "Fluency, Muteness and Commitment in Camus's *La Peste*." *French Studies* 34 (1980): 422–33.

Grenier, Jean. "Santa Cruz." In his *Inspirations méditerranéennes*. Paris: Gallimard, 1961, 15–20.

Grobe, Edwin P. "Camus and the Parable of the Perfect Sentence." *Symposium* 24 (1970): 254–61.

Guérin, Daniel. "L'Anarchisme. Collection Idées. Paris: Gallimard, 1970.

Guide de la ville d'Oran. By the Œuvres Sociales de la Mutuelle Générale de la Sûreté, National d'Oran. Oran: Imprimérie de la Lyre, n.d.

Haggis, Donald. *Camus:* La Peste. Woodbury: Barron's, 1962.

Hallie, Philip P. *Lest Innocent Blood Be Shed: The Story of the Village of Le Chambon, and How Goodness Happened There.* New York: Harper, 1979.

Harvey, Paul, and J. E. Heseltine. *The Oxford Companion to French Literature.* Oxford: Clarendon, 1969.

Heggoy, Alf Andrew. *Historical Dictionary of Algeria.* Metuchen: Scarecrow, 1981.

Hirst, L. Fabian. *The Conquest of Plague: A Study of the Evolution of Epidemiology.* Oxford: Clarendon, 1953.

Hollahan, Eugene. "The Path of Sympathy: Abstraction and Imagination in Camus's *La Peste.*" *Studies in the Novel* 8 (1976): 377–93.

Jayne, Walter Addison. *The Healing Gods of Ancient Civilizations.* 1925. New York: University Books, 1962.

Joyeux, Maurice. *L'Anarchie et la société moderne.* Paris: Nouvelles Editions Debresse, 1969.

Kaufmann, Walter. *Existentialism from Dostoevsky to Sartre.* New York: Meridian, 1957.

Kellman, Steven G. "Singular Third Person: Camus' *La Peste.*" *Kentucky Romance Quarterly* 25 (1978): 499–507.

Klemke, E. D. *The Meaning of Life.* New York: Oxford Univ. Press, 1981.

Knight, Everett W. *Literature Considered as Philosophy.* New York: Collier, 1962.

Landa, Louis, introd. *A Journal of the Plague Year.* By Daniel Defoe. New York: Oxford Univ. Press, 1969.

Lazere, Donald. "American Criticism of the Sartre-Camus Dispute." In *The Philosophy of Jean-Paul Sartre.* Ed. Paul A. Schilpp. La Salle: Open Court, 1981, 408–21.

———. *The Unique Creation of Albert Camus.* New Haven: Yale Univ. Press, 1973.

Lespès, René. *Oran: Etude de géographie et d'histoire urbaine.* Collection du Centenaire de l'Algérie 1830–1938. Paris: Alcan, 1938.

Lévi-Valensi, J., ed. *Albert Camus et les critiques de notre temps.* Paris: Garnier, 1970.

———. "Le Temps et l'espace dans l'œuvre romanesque de Camus." In Gay-Crosier, *Camus* 57–68.

Lottman, Herbert R. *Albert Camus.* Paris: Editions de Seuil, 1977.

———. *Albert Camus: A Biography.* Garden City: Doubleday, 1979.

———. *The Left Bank: Writers, Artists, and Politics from the Popular Front to the Cold War.* Boston: Houghton, 1982.

Madaule, Jacques. *Histoire de France.* Collection Idées. Paris: Gallimard, 1966.

Maitron, Jean. *Histoire du mouvement anarchiste en France (1880–1914).* Paris: Société Universitaire, 1951.

Maquet, Albert. *Albert Camus; ou, L'invincible été*. Paris: Nouvelles Editions Debresse, 1956.

———. *Albert Camus: The Invincible Summer*. Trans. Herma Briffault. 1958. New York: Humanities, 1972.

McCarthy, Patrick. *Camus*. New York: Random, 1982.

McNeill, William H. *Plagues and People*. Garden City: Doubleday, 1976.

Merskey, H., and F. G. Spear. *Pain: Psychological and Physical Aspects*. London: Bailliere, 1967.

Merton, Thomas. *Albert Camus'* The Plague: *Introduction and Commentary by Thomas Merton*. New York: Seabury, 1968.

Michel, Henri. *Histoire de la Résistance en France*. 5th ed. Paris: Presses Universitaires, 1969.

Morier, Henri. *Dictionnaire de poétique et de rhétorique*. 2nd ed. Paris: Presses Universitaires, 1975.

Nadeau, Maurice. *Le Roman français depuis la guerre*. Paris: Gallimard, 1970.

Nohl, Johannes. *The Black Death*. Trans. C. H. Clarke. 1924. New York: Humanities, 1961.

Ober, William B., and Nabil Alloush. "The Plague at Granada, 1348–1349: Ibn Al-Khatib and Ideas of Contagion." *Bulletin of the New York Academy of Medicine*, 2nd ser., 58 (1982): 418–24.

O'Brien, Conor Cruise. *Albert Camus of Europe and Africa*. New York: Viking, 1970.

Onimus, Jean. *Albert Camus and Christianity* (trans. of *Camus*). Trans. Emmett Parker. University: University of Alabama Press, 1970.

———. *Camus*. Paris: Desclée, De Brouwer, 1965.

Parry, Adam. "The Language of Thucydides' Description of the Plague." *London Institute of Classical Studies Bulletin* 16 (1969): 106–18.

Paxton, Robert O. *Vichy France: Old Guard and New Order*. New York: Knopf, 1972.

Peyre, Henri. *French Novelists of Today*. New York: Oxford Univ. Press, 1967.

Pilla, Francesco di. *Albert Camus e la critica: Bibliografia internazionale (1937–1971), con un saggio introduttivo*. Lecce: Milella, 1973.

Ponge, Francis. *Le Parti-Pris des choses*. Paris: Gallimard, 1942.

Porter, Burton F. *Philosophy: A Literary and Conceptual Approach*. 2nd ed. New York: Harcourt, 1980.

Prince, Gerald J. "Le Discours attributif dans *La Peste*." *Albert Camus, 1980*, ed. Raymond Gay-Crosier, 101–09.

Proust, Achille Adrien. *La Défense de l'Europe contre la peste et la Conférence de Venise de 1897*. Paris: Masson, 1897.

Puget, Jean-Loup. "Perspectives de l'anarchie." *La Rue* No. 5 (1969): 27–34.

Quilliot, Roger. *The Sea and Prisons: A Commentary on the Life and Thought of Albert Camus*. Trans. Emmett Parker. University: Univ. of Alabama Press, 1970.

————. *La Mer et les prisons: Essai sur Albert Camus.* Paris: Gallimard, 1956.

Rank, Otto. *The Double.* Trans. Harry Tucker, Jr. Chapel Hill: Univ. of North Carolina Press, 1971.

Rhein, Phillip H. *Albert Camus.* New York: Twayne, 1969.

Robbe-Grillet, Alain. *For a New Novel: Essays on Fiction.* Trans. Richard Howard. New York: Grove, 1965.

————. *Pour un noveau roman.* Paris: Editions de Minuit, 1963.

Roblès, Emmanuel. "La Marque du Soleil et de la misère." In *Camus.* [By René Marill Albérès et al.] Paris: Hachette, 1964.

Roeming, Robert F. *Camus: A Bibliography.* Madison: Univ. of Wisconsin Press, 1968.

Rolland, Romain. "Au-dessus de la mêlée." In his *L'Esprit Libre.* Paris: Albin Michel, 1953, 60–178.

Romains, Jules. *Knock.* Paris: Gallimard, 1923.

————. *Mort de quelqu'un.* Paris: Gallimard, 1924.

Rousselot, Jean. "Nostalgie d'Oran." *Algérie et l'Afrique de Nord* 16, NS No. 2 (1948): 13–15.

Roy, Jules. *La Guerre d'Algérie.* Paris: R. Julliard, 1960.

————. *The War in Algeria.* Trans. Richard Howard. 1961. Westport: Greenwood, 1975.

Sanders, Steven, and David R. Cheney, eds. *The Meaning of Life: Questions, Answers and Analysis.* Englewood Cliffs: Prentice, 1980.

Sartre, Jean-Paul. *Situations II.* Paris: Gallimard, 1948.

Shirer, William L. *The Rise and Fall of the Third Reich.* New York: Simon, 1960.

Shrewsbury, J. F. D. *A History of Bubonic Plague in the British Isles.* London: Cambridge Univ. Press, 1970.

Sigerist, Henry E. *Civilization and Disease.* Chicago: Univ. of Chicago Press, 1962.

————. "Paracelsus in the Light of Four Hundred Years." In his *On the History of Medicine.* New York: MD, 1960, 162–76.

Smith, Geddes. *Plague on Us.* New York: Commonwealth Fund, 1943.

Solomon, Robert C., ed. *Existentialism.* New York: Random, 1974.

Sontag, Susan. *Illness as Metaphor.* New York: Farrar, 1978.

Spanos, William V., ed. *Casebook on Existentialism Two.* New York: Crowell, 1976.

Suleiman, Susan. "Le Récit exemplaire: Parabole, fable, roman à thèse." *Poétique* 32 (1977): 468–89.

————. "Redundancy and the 'Readable' Text." *Poetics Today* 1 (1980): 119–42.

————, and Inge Crossman, eds. *The Reader in the Text: Essays on Audience and Interpretation.* Princeton: Princeton Univ. Press, 1980.

Tharpe, Jac, ed. *Art and Ethics: A Collection of Essays on Percy.* Oxford: Univ. Press of Mississippi, 1980.

Thody, Philip. *Albert Camus: A Study of His Work.* New York: Grove, 1959.

————. *Albert Camus 1913–1960*. New York: Macmillan, 1961.

Thomas, Lewis. "The Art of Teaching Science." *New York Times Magazine*, 14 March 1982, 89–93.

Thorndike, Lynn. *A History of Magic and Experimental Science*. New York: Columbia Univ. Press, 1934.

Tompkins, Jane P., ed. *Reader-Response Criticism: From Formalism to Post-Structuralism*. Baltimore: Johns Hopkins Univ. Press, 1980.

Tuchman, Barbara. *A Distant Mirror: The Calamitous Fourteenth Century*. New York: Knopf, 1978.

Werner, E. T. C. *Myths and Legends of China*. London: Harrap, 1922.

Wilkinson, James D. *The Intellectual Resistance in Europe*. Cambridge: Harvard Univ. Press, 1981.

Willhoite, Fred H., Jr. *Beyond Nihilism: Albert Camus's Contribution to Political Thought*. Baton Rouge: Louisiana State Univ. Press, 1968.

Wright, Gordon. *France in Modern Times*. 3rd ed. New York: Norton, 1981.

Ziegler, Philip. *The Black Death*. New York: Harper, 1969.

Recordings, Filmstrips, and Films

Bantz, Judith, prod. *Albert Camus*. Sound filmstrip. Schloat Productions, 1973.

Camus, Albert. *Albert Camus Reading in French*. Caedmon TC 1138, 1960.

Kazan, Elia, dir. *Panic in the Streets*. Twentieth Century Fox, 1950.

Klise, Thomas S., prod., writer, and narrator. *Albert Camus*. Sound filmstrip. Thomas S. Klise Co., 1972.

Orjain, Fred, prod. *Albert Camus: A Self-Portrait*. Sound filmstrip. Learning Corp. of America, 1972.

Pontecorvo, Gillo, dir. *La Battaglia di Algeri*. Igor Films S. r. l., 1966.

Villiers, François, dir. *Le Foulard de Smyrne*. Films Jean Giono, 1958.

Visconti, Luchino, dir. *L'Etranger*. Paramount, 1967.

INDEX